How to access your online resources

Kaplan Financial students will have a MyKaplan account and these extra resources will be available to you online. You do not need to register again, as this process was completed when you enrolled. If you are having problems accessing online materials, please ask your course administrator.

If you are not studying with Kaplan and did not purchase your book via a Kaplan website, to unlock your extra online resources please go to **www.en-gage.co.uk** (even if you have set up an account and registered books previously). You will then need to enter the ISBN number (on the title page and back cover) and the unique pass key number contained in the scratch panel below to gain access.

You will also be required to enter additional information during this process to set up or confirm your account details.

If you purchased through the Kaplan Publishing website you will automatically receive an e-mail invitation to register your details and gain access to your content. If you do not receive the e-mail or book content, please contact Kaplan Publishing.

This code can only be used once for the registration of this book online. This registration and your online content will expire when the examinations covered by this book have taken place. Please allow one hour from the time you submit your book details for us to process your request.

Please scratch the film to access your unique code.

Please be aware that this code is case-sensitive and you will need to include the dashes within the passcode, but not when entering the ISBN.

KAPLAN
PUBLISHING

CIMA's CGMA® 2019 Professional Examinations

CIMA's CGMA Strategic Level

Subject P3

Risk Management

EXAM PRACTICE KIT

CIMA®

KAPLAN

PUBLISHING

British Library Cataloguing-in-Publication Data

A catalogue record for this book is available from the British Library.

Published by:

Kaplan Publishing UK
Unit 2 The Business Centre
Molly Millar's Lane
Wokingham
Berkshire
RG41 2QZ

ISBN: 978-1-83996-791-7

© Kaplan Financial Limited, 2024

Kaplan Publishing's learning materials are designed to help students succeed in their examinations. In certain circumstances, CIMA can make post-exam adjustment to a student's mark or grade to reflect adverse circumstances which may have disadvantaged a student's ability to take an exam or demonstrate their normal level of attainment (see CIMA's Special Consideration policy). However, it should be noted that students will not be eligible for special consideration by CIMA if preparation for or performance in CIMA's exam are affected by any failure by their tuition provider to prepare them properly for the exam for any reason including, but not limited to, staff shortages, building work or a lack of facilities etc.

Similarly, CIMA will not accept applications for special consideration on any of the following grounds:

- failure by a tuition provider to cover the whole syllabus

- failure by the student to cover the whole syllabus, for instance as a result of joining a course part way through

- failure by the student to prepare adequately for the exam, or to use the correct pre-seen material

- errors in the Kaplan Official Study Text, including sample (practice) questions or any other Kaplan content or

- errors in any other study materials (from any other tuition provider or publisher).

CONTENTS

Section

Quality and accuracy are of the utmost importance to us so if you spot an error in any of our products, please send an email to mykaplanreporting@kaplan.com with full details.

Our Quality Co-ordinator will work with our technical team to verify the error and take action to ensure it is corrected in future editions.

P.4

INDEX TO QUESTIONS AND ANSWERS

OBJECTIVE TEST QUESTIONS

EXAM TECHNIQUES

COMPUTER-BASED ASSESSMENT

Golden rules

1   Make sure you have completed the compulsory 15-minute tutorial before you start the test. This tutorial is available through the AICPA & CIMA website and focusses on the functionality of the exam. You cannot speak to the invigilator once you have started.

2   These exam practice kits give you plenty of exam style questions to practise so make sure you use them to fully prepare.

3   Attempt all questions, there is no negative marking.

4   Double check your answer before you put in the final answer although you can change your response as many times as you like.

5   Not all questions will be multiple choice questions (MCQs) – you may have to fill in missing words or figures.

6   Identify the easy questions first and get some points on the board to build up your confidence.

7   Attempt 'wordy' questions first as these may be quicker than the computation style questions. This will relieve some of the time pressure you will be under during the exam.

8   If you don't know the answer, flag the question and attempt it later. In your final review before the end of the exam try a process of elimination.

9   Work out your answer on the whiteboard provided first if it is easier for you. There is also an onscreen 'scratch pad' on which you can make notes. You are not allowed to take pens, pencils, rulers, pencil cases, phones, paper or notes into the testing room.

SYLLABUS GUIDANCE, LEARNING OBJECTIVES AND VERBS

A   CIMA's CGMA® 2019 PROFESSIONAL QUALIFICATION

Details regarding the content of CIMA's CGMA 2019 Professional Qualification can be located within the CGMA 2019 Professional Qualification syllabus document.

You can use the following diagram showing the whole structure of your qualification to help you keep track of your progress. Make sure you seek appropriate advice if you are unsure about your progression through the qualification.

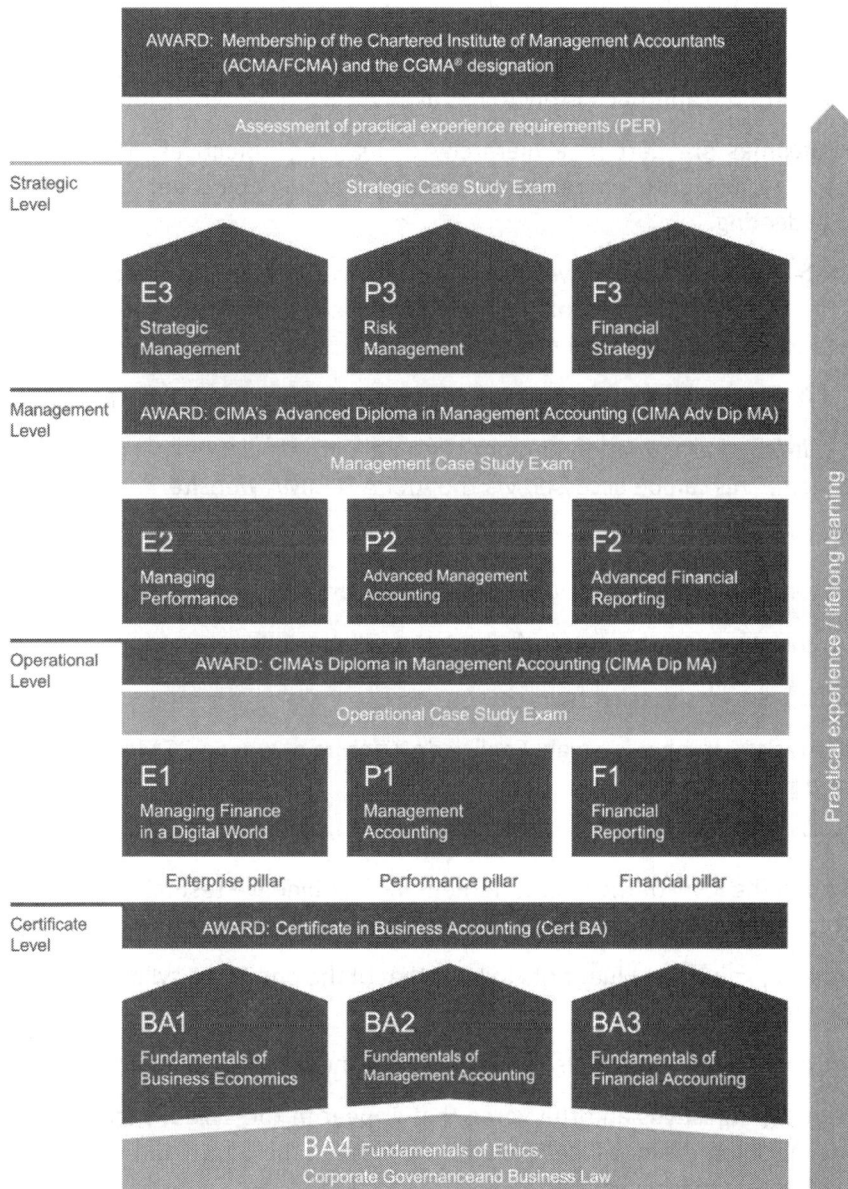

Reproduced with CIMA's permission

B STUDY WEIGHTINGS

A percentage weighting is shown against each exam content area in CIMA's CGMA® Exam Blueprints. This is intended as a guide to the proportion of study time each topic requires.

All component learning outcomes will be tested.

The weightings do not specify the number of marks that will be allocated to topics in the examination.

C LEARNING OUTCOMES

Each subject within the qualification is divided into a number of broad syllabus topics. The topics contain one or more lead learning outcomes, related component learning outcomes and indicative knowledge content.

A learning outcome has two main purposes:

1   to define the skill or ability that a well-prepared candidate should be able to exhibit in the examination

2   to demonstrate the approach likely to be taken by examiners in examination questions.

The learning outcomes are part of a hierarchy of learning objectives. The verbs used at the beginning of each learning outcome relate to a specific learning objective, e.g. Evaluate alternative approaches to budgeting.

The verb 'evaluate' indicates a high-level learning objective. As learning objectives are hierarchical, it is expected that at this level students will have knowledge of different budgeting systems and methodologies and be able to apply them.

CIMA's CGMA Exam Blueprints and representative task statements

CIMA has also published examination blueprints giving learners clear expectations regarding what is expected of them. This can be accessed via the AICPA & CIMA website.

The blueprint is structured as follows:

• Exam content sections (reflecting the syllabus document)

• Lead and component outcomes (reflecting the syllabus document)

• Representative task statements.

A representative task statement is a plain English description of what a CGMA® finance professional should know and be able to do.

The content and skill level determine the language and verbs used in the representative task.

CIMA will test up to the level of the task statement in the objective test (an objective test question on a particular topic could be set at a lower level than the task statement in the blueprint).

The format of the objective test blueprints follows that of the published syllabus for the 2019 CGMA Professional Qualification.

Weightings for content sections are also included in the individual subject blueprints.

A list of the learning objectives and the verbs that appear in the syllabus learning outcomes and examinations follows and these will help you to understand the depth and breadth required for a topic and the skill level the topic relates to.

CIMA's verb hierarchy

Skill level	Verbs used	Definition
Level 5 **Evaluation** How you are expected to use your learning to evaluate, make decisions or recommendations	Advise	Counsel, inform or notify
	Assess	Evaluate or estimate the nature, ability or quality of
	Evaluate	Appraise or assess the value of
	Recommend	Propose a course of action
	Review	Assess and evaluate in order, to change if necessary
Level 4 **Analysis** How you are expected to analyse the detail of what you have learned	Align	Arrange in an orderly way
	Analyse	Examine in detail the structure of
	Communicate	Share or exchange information
	Compare and contrast	Show the similarities and/or differences between
	Develop	Grow and expand a concept
	Discuss	Examine in detail by argument
	Examine	Inspect thoroughly
	Interpret	Translate into intelligible or familiar terms
	Monitor	Observe and check the progress of
	Prioritise	Place in order of priority or sequence for action
	Produce	Create or bring into existence
Level 3 **Application** How you are expected to apply your knowledge	Apply	Put to practical use
	Calculate	Ascertain or reckon mathematically
	Conduct	Organise and carry out
	Demonstrate	Prove with certainty or exhibit by practical means
	Prepare	Make or get ready for use
	Reconcile	Make or prove consistent/compatible
Level 2 **Comprehension** What you are expected to understand	Describe	Communicate the key features of
	Distinguish	Highlight the differences between
	Explain	Make clear or intelligible/state the meaning or purpose of
	Identify	Recognise, establish or select after consideration
	Illustrate	Use an example to describe or explain something
Level 1 **Knowledge** What you are expected to know	List	Make a list of
	State	Express, fully or clearly, the details/facts of
	Define	Give the exact meaning of
	Outline	Give a summary of

D   OBJECTIVE TEST

Objective test

Objective test questions require you to choose or provide a response to a question whose correct answer is predetermined.

The most common types of objective test question you will see are:

- Multiple choice, where you have to choose the correct answer(s) from a list of possible answers. This could either be numbers or text.

- Multiple response, for example, choosing two correct answers from a list of eight possible answers. This could either be numbers or text.

- Fill in the blank, where you fill in your answer within the provided space.

- Drag and drop, for example, matching a technical term with the correct definition.

- Hot spots, where you select an answer by clicking on graphs/diagrams.

Guidance on CIMA's on-screen calculator

As part of the CGMA Objective Test software, candidates are now provided with a calculator. This calculator is on-screen and is available for the duration of the assessment. The calculator is available in each of the Objective Tests and is accessed by clicking the calculator button in the top left hand corner of the screen at any time during the assessment. Candidates are permitted to utilise personal calculators as long as they are an approved CIMA model. CIMA approved model list can be found on the AICPA & CIMA website.

All candidates must complete a 15-minute exam tutorial before the assessment begins and will have the opportunity to familiarise themselves with the calculator and practise using it. The exam tutorial is also available online via the AICPA & CIMA website. Candidates can use their own calculators providing it is included in CIMA's authorised calculator listing.

Fundamentals of objective tests

The objective tests are 90-minute assessments comprising 60 compulsory questions, with one or more parts. There will be no choice and all questions should be attempted. All elements of a question must be answered correctly for the question to be marked correctly. All questions are equally weighted.

APPROACH TO REVISION

Stage 1: Assess areas of strengths and weaknesses

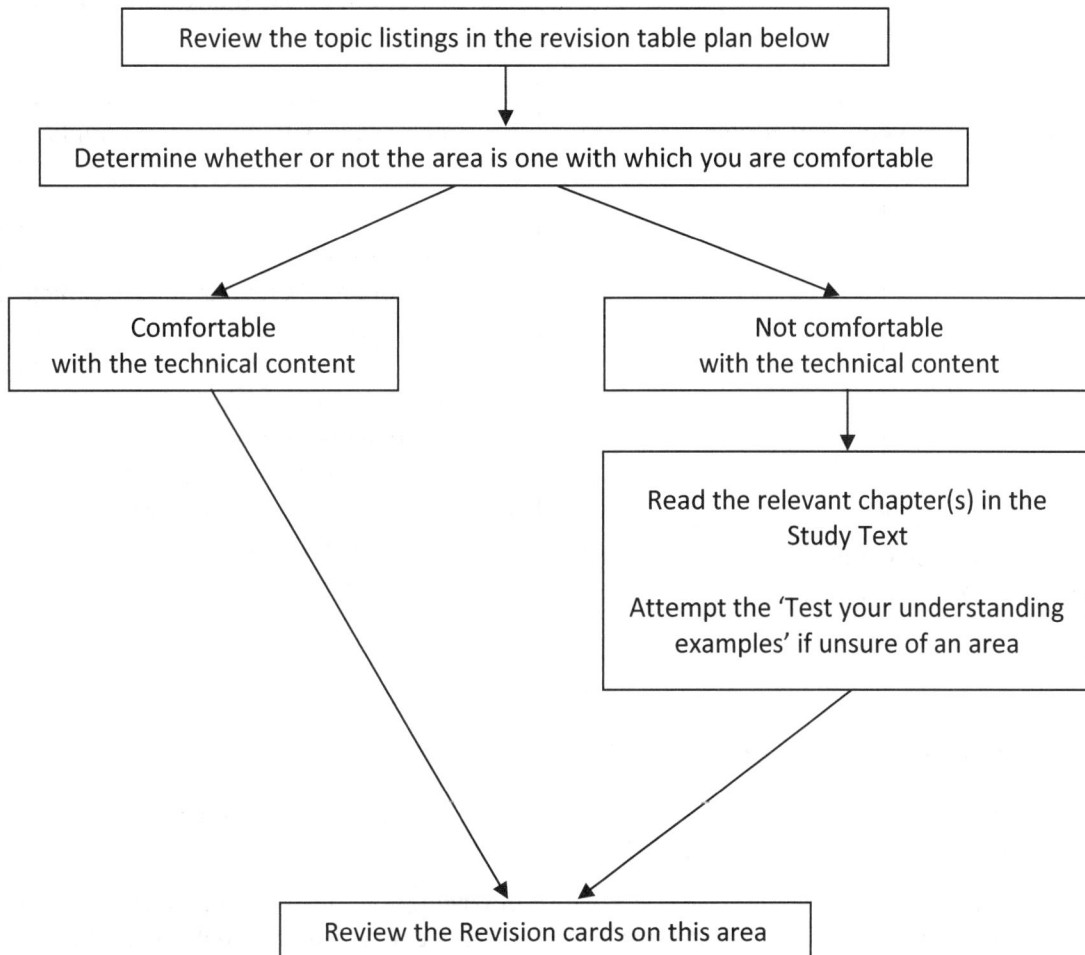

```
┌─────────────────────────────────────────────────────────┐
│   Review the topic listings in the revision table plan below │
└─────────────────────────────────────────────────────────┘
                              │
                              ▼
┌─────────────────────────────────────────────────────────┐
│ Determine whether or not the area is one with which you are comfortable │
└─────────────────────────────────────────────────────────┘
```

```
┌──────────────────────┐          ┌──────────────────────┐
│     Comfortable      │          │    Not comfortable    │
│ with the technical content │     │ with the technical content │
└──────────────────────┘          └──────────────────────┘
                                              │
                                              ▼
                                   ┌──────────────────────────┐
                                   │ Read the relevant chapter(s) in the │
                                   │        Study Text         │
                                   │                          │
                                   │ Attempt the 'Test your understanding │
                                   │ examples' if unsure of an area │
                                   └──────────────────────────┘
```

```
              ┌──────────────────────────────────────┐
              │   Review the Revision cards on this area   │
              └──────────────────────────────────────┘
```

Stage 2: Question practice

Follow the order of revision of topics as recommended in the revision table plan below and attempt the questions in the order suggested.

Try to avoid referring to textbooks and notes and the model answer until you have completed your attempt.

Try to answer the question in the allotted time.

Review your attempt with the model answer and assess how much of the answer you achieved in the allocated exam time.

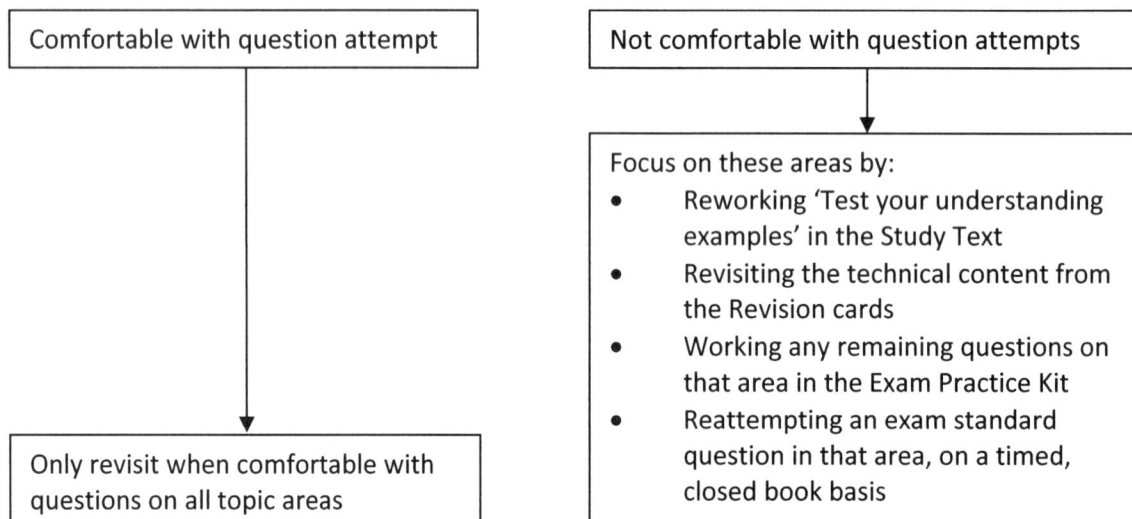

Comfortable with question attempt

Not comfortable with question attempts

Focus on these areas by:
- Reworking 'Test your understanding examples' in the Study Text
- Revisiting the technical content from the Revision cards
- Working any remaining questions on that area in the Exam Practice Kit
- Reattempting an exam standard question in that area, on a timed, closed book basis

Only revisit when comfortable with questions on all topic areas

Stage 3: Final pre-exam revision

We recommend that you **attempt at least one ninety minute mock examination** containing a set of previously unseen exam standard questions.

It is important that you get a feel for the breadth of coverage of a real exam without advanced knowledge of the topic areas covered – just as you will expect to see on the real exam day.

Ideally a mock examination offered by your tuition provider should be sat in timed, closed book, real exam conditions.

CGMA SYLLABUS GRIDS

P3: Risk Management

Analyse, evaluate and manage strategic, operational and cyber risks

Content weighting

	Content area	Weighting
A	Enterprise risk	25%
B	Strategic risk	25%
C	Internal controls	25%
D	Cyber risk	25%
		100%

P3A: Enterprise risk

Not all intended strategies are implemented due to various factors. These factors constitute the operating enterprise-wide risks of the organisation. This section covers how to identify, evaluate and manage these risks.

Lead outcome	Component outcome	Topics to be covered	Explanatory notes
1. Analyse sources and types of risk.	Analyse: a. Sources of risks b. Types of risks	• Upside and downside risks • Risks arising from internal and external sources • Risks arising from international operations • Strategic and operational risks	What are the types and sources of risks that would prevent organisations from implementing their intended strategy?
2. Evaluate risk.	a. Evaluate the impact of risk b. Assess the likelihood of risks c. Analyse the interaction of different risks	• Quantification of risk exposure • Risk maps	What is the impact of the risks on the organisation? What techniques are available to evaluate the impact of such risks?
3. Discuss ways of managing risks.	Discuss: a. Roles and responsibilities b. Risk tolerance, appetite and capacity c. Risk management frameworks d. Risk analytics	• Role of board and others in the organisation for identifying and managing risks • Risk mitigation including TARA – transfer, avoid, reduce, accept • Assurance mapping • Risk register • Risk reports and responses • Ethical dilemmas associated with risk management	How is risk managed in the organisation? How is responsibility for various aspects of risk management distributed in the organisation? How does the organisation align its risk tolerance, appetite and capacity to its decisions and actions? What risk management frameworks are there? How is risk information communicated to the organisation?

P3B: Strategic risk

A fundamental risk of the organisation is that its strategy is the wrong one and that even if implemented perfectly, it will achieve the wrong outcome for the organisation. In addition, some risks are of such high significance that they can affect the very existence of the organisation. This section covers where these risks emanate from, evaluates them and explains how oversight of such risks is critical to the governance of the organisation.

Lead outcome	Component outcome	Topics to be covered	Explanatory notes
1. Analyse risks associated with formulating strategy.	a. Analyse relevance of the assumptions on which strategy is based. b. Discuss potential sources and types of disruptions to strategy.	• Analysis of strategic choice • Scenario planning • Stress-testing strategy	What are the risks that the strategy of the organisation is wrong? What are the sources of such risks? How does the organisation evolve its strategy in a dynamic environment to keep it relevant?
2. Evaluate the sources and impact of reputational risks.	Evaluate: a. Sources of reputational risk b. Impact of reputational risk on strategy	• Risks of unethical behaviour • Impact on brand and reputation of organisation	What is reputational risk and why is it an important strategic risk? What are the types and sources of reputational risks and what is their impact on the organisation? How can they be managed?
3. Explain governance risks.	Explain: a. The role of board and its committees in managing strategic risk b. Failure of governance and its impact on strategy	• Separation of the roles of CEO and chairman • Role of non-executive directors • Roles of audit committee, remuneration committee, risk committee and nomination committee • Directors' remuneration	What is the role of the board in risk management? How does governance risk occur? How is this role governed by the various corporate governance codes and principles?

P3C: Internal controls

Control systems are an integral part of managing risks. Various control frameworks have been developed to assist in this process. In addition, the internal audit function performs a vital role in helping to implement and monitor implementation and adherence to the control frameworks. This section covers how internal control systems can be used effectively in the risk management process.

Lead outcome	Component outcome	Topics to be covered	Explanatory notes
1. Analyse internal control systems.	a. Discuss roles and responsibilities for internal controls. b. Discuss the purpose of internal control. c. Analyse the features of internal control systems.	• Role of risk manager as distinct from internal auditor • Control systems in functional areas • Operational features of internal control	What are the roles of internal control systems in managing risks? What are its key features and why?
2. Recommend internal controls for risk management.	a. Discuss the Committee of Sponsoring Organisations of the Treadway Commission (COSO) internal control and risk management framework. b. Assess control weakness. c. Assess compliance failures. d. Recommend internal controls for risk management.	• Governance and culture • Strategy and objective setting • Performance • Review and revision • Information, communication and reporting • Identifying and evaluating control weakness and compliance failures	This introduces the COSO framework as a comprehensive way of looking at internal controls in risk management. The objective is to get candidates to understand the key elements and know how to apply them in evaluating internal controls.
3. Discuss various issues relating to internal audit in organisations.	Discuss: a. Forms of internal audit b. Internal audit process c. Effective internal audit d. The internal audit report	• Compliance audit, fraud investigation, value for money audit and management audit • Operation of internal audit • Assessment of audit risk • Process of analytical review • Independence, staffing and resourcing of internal audit • Preparation and interpretation of internal audit reports	This part looks at the critical role that the internal audit function can play in risk management. The objective is to create awareness and understanding of the various issues in internal audit and how they link to each other.

P3D: Cyber risks

In a digital world one of the major threats is cyber risk. How are data and operating systems protected from unauthorised access and manipulation? How are breaches identified, analysed, remedied and reported? These are some of the questions covered in this section.

Lead outcome	Component outcome	Topics to be covered	Explanatory notes
1. Analyse cyber threats.	Analyse: a. Nature and impact of cyber risks b. Types of cyber risks c. Risk of security vulnerabilities.	• Malware • Application attacks • Hackers • Result of vulnerabilities including downtime, reputational loss, customer flight, legal and industry consequences	This part looks at where and how organisations can be vulnerable to cyber threats and the type and sources of such threats. In addition, it looks at the impact such threats can have on organisations.
2. Review cyber security processes.	Review: a. Cyber security objectives b. Security controls c. Centralisation in cyber security	• Protection, detection and response • Centralised management • Centralised monitoring	The principal aim here is to enable candidates to understand how to manage cyber threats through cyber security processes. What objectives should organisations set in this area? What controls are available to organisations?
3. Discuss cyber security tools and techniques.	Discuss: a. Forensic analysis b. Malware analysis c. Penetration testing d. Software security	• System level analysis, storage analysis and network analysis • Reverse engineering, decompilation and disassembly • Network discovery, vulnerability probing, exploiting vulnerabilities • Tiers of software security	This part looks at the tools and techniques available to manage cyber risks. Candidates are expected to have a basic understanding of the techniques and how they can be deployed together.
4. Evaluate cyber risk reporting.	a. Evaluate cyber risk reporting frameworks	• Description criteria including nature of business and operations, nature of information at risk, risk management programme objectives, cybersecurity risk governance structure etc.	How should cyber risks be reported? What reporting frameworks are available?

Information concerning formulae and tables will be provided via the CIMA website, www.aicpa-cima.com

Section 1

OBJECTIVE TEST QUESTIONS

ENTERPRISE RISK

1   Which one of the following sentences best describes risk?

A   The exposure to the adverse consequences of dangerous environments

B   The expected impact of uncertain future events on objectives

C   The chance of being caught doing something unethical

D   The impact of the exposure to the adverse consequences of uncertain future events

2   Risk management is the process of reducing the adverse consequences either by reducing the _____ of an event or its _____.

What are the two missing words?

A   Understanding and impact

B   Likelihood and potential

C   Understanding and potential

D   Likelihood and impact

3   Risk appetite is determined by

A   Risk attitude and risk awareness

B   Risk attitude and risk capacity

C   Risk strategy and risk awareness

D   Risk attitude and residual risk

4   The four strategies in TARA for managing risk do NOT include which one of the following?

A   Transference

B   Approval

C   Avoidance

D   Acceptance

5   Risks can be categorised as either 'pure' or 'speculative'. Drag and drop the following risks into the correct category.

	Pure risks	Speculative risks
The risk that a fire may destroy company assets		
The risk that a customer goes out of business		
The risk that a foreign exchange rate may change		
The risk relating to the level of future profits		
The risk that a capital investment may not yield the predicted IRR		
The risk that a virus is introduced to a computer application		

6   There are six steps in CIMA's risk management cycle. Identify the correct sequence of steps, by entering step numbers below.

Development of risk response strategy	
Implement strategy and allocate responsibilities	
Review and refine process and do it again	
Identify risk areas	
Implementation and monitoring of controls	
Understand and assess scale of risk	

7   Match each of the following risks to the appropriate risk category.

Risk category	Risk
Business risks	Inflation rate rises
Economic risks	Exchange rate changes
Environmental risks	Failure of a new product
Financial risks	Rate of climate change increases

8   Match each of the following risks to the appropriate risk category.

Risk category	Risk
Business risks	CEO convicted of insider dealing
Economic risks	Disposable income levels fall
Corporate reputation risks	Nationalisation of industry
Political risks	Raw material prices rise

9   **Match each of the following risks to the appropriate risk category.**

Risk category	Risk
Political risks	Government increases rate of Corporation Tax
Legal risks	Company prosecuted for breach of the Data Protection Act
Regulatory risks	Change of Government
Compliance risks	Customer sues company for negligence

10   **X is a food manufacturer. X uses genetically modified (GM) ingredients in some of its products. A change in public opinion regarding GM foods represents which of the following types of risk? (One only)**

A   Business risk

B   Economic risk

C   Reputation risk

D   Environmental risk

11   AA plc is a multinational company, retailing household electrical appliances. The finance director is concerned about the lack of risk management as at the present time AA plc only look at financial risk.

Select THREE of the following risk categories that would also be relevant for AA plc to assess:

A   Gearing

B   Product risk

C   Reputation risk

D   Risk response

E   Technological risk

F   Monitoring Risk

12   Viva plc is a large casino company, operating all over the world. Each casino is a multi-million pound construction project. Viva plc's current policy is to finance expansion using high debt levels.

Which THREE of the following risks would you identify as critical for Viva to assess?

A   Financial risk

B   Project risk

C   Foreign Exchange rate risk

D   Production risk

E   Health and safety risk

F   commodity price risk

13   OKJ is currently undertaking a risk analysis.

Which TWO of the following factors are the most important risk issues facing OKJ?

A   OKJ's home country has recently elected a new government. It is not yet clear if they will introduce new legislation to increase minimum wages. This would have a major impact on OKJ's profitability.

B   After a recent accident in one of its factories, OKJ was convicted of breaching relevant health and safety legislation. Based on similar recent cases brought in the industry, OKJ expects to be fined around 7% of its turnover. OKJ has insurance in place that will cover this fine.

C   OKJ uses platinum as a key component within some of its products. The price of metals varies significantly on world markets and tends to rise sharply in times of recession. The directors are concerned that its products may become unprofitable if platinum prices rise more than 20% from their current levels, but is uncertain about whether this would happen – even if a recession does occur.

D   OKJ is uncertain about whether it can retain its CEO in the long term. It has had a number of CEO's over the last five years – each of them staying very different lengths of time in their roles. Fortunately, OKJ has an experienced Board of Directors and the change in CEOs has had little impact on the business in the past.

14   **One of the first steps in developing a risk management strategy is to determine the risk capacity, attitude and appetite of the organisation. Match the definitions with the terms below:**

Term	Definition
risk capacity	'the overall approach to risk'
risk attitude	'the amount of risk that the organisation is willing to accept in the pursuit of value added'
risk appetite	'the amount of risk that the organisation is able to bear'

15   **The Board of X is discussing risk. The first item for discussion is the organisation's 'risk appetite'. Which of the following factors determine the risk appetite of an organisation?**

Select ALL that apply.

A   The background of the board

B   The number of directors

C   The reputation of X

D   The nature of the product or service of X

E   Customer expectations

16 The identification of risk is an important stage in developing a risk management strategy. Approaches to identifying risk are categorised as internal or external, and proactive or reactive.

The use of SWOT and PEST(EL) analysis are both examples of which approach?

A   internal proactive

B   internal reactive

C   external proactive

D   external reactive

17 'Be A Sport Ltd' is a medium-sized event organiser and is considering the following four possible strategies and how best to manage the risks involved:

1   A race event Be A Sport Ltd has organised for next week is an outdoors 5k run. However if it rains it is unlikely to attract enough competitors to make any profit. The management have decided to still hold the event.

2   Be A Sport Ltd has just taken out a large insurance contract to ensure they are covered if any competitor seeks damages for injuries caused in one of their races.

3   One of the employees at Be A Sport Ltd has had an innovative idea to hold a waterfall jumping event where competitors compete to jump from the highest possible place along a sheer cliff edge into the North Sea. After considering the idea the Be A Sport Ltd management have rejected it as it is too dangerous.

4   As part of the organisation of the huge annual showcase event Be A Sport Ltd hold, they have conducted a large and extensive risk assessment process and put into place all the internal controls they believe to be necessary.

Match the strategy that best fits the following four risk management methods?

Risk Management Method	Strategy
Transfer	
Accept	
Reduce	
Avoid	

18 X is a company involved in oil exploration and extraction. Following a risk review, X has identified that earthquakes occur in its exploration areas once every five years, on average. The average cost of work to resume oil production, following an earthquake, is estimated to be US$ 30million.

Calculate the value of the risk of earthquakes, in US$, to the nearest million.

19 Political risk analysis is conducted by a company considering international operations.

Which ONE of the following is the normal focus of this analysis?

A   world economy generally

B   relations between the USA, Japan and Europe

C   political and cultural differences between the home and target country

D   industrialisation of the target country

20 D, a finance manager, has been asked to forecast the sales for next year. The standard calculation with the organisation is to account for various probable outcomes using expected values. D has been given the following information by the Sales Manager

Forecast sales for next year	Probability of occurrence
£200,000	10%
£250,000	40%
£300,000	30%
£350,000	20%

Calculate which ONE of the following is the EXPECTED value of sales for next year?

A   £200,000

B   £260,000

C   £280,000

D   £240,000

21 Party Ltd is a successful family-run business retailing party ware from a small shop in the UK. The younger members of the business wish to open another larger shop in a neighbouring town and to expand into e-business, selling across the country via the Internet. However, the Managing Director, founder and mother of the younger family members has resisted all change and says that the business is doing fine without any change, so there is no reason to do anything.

Which ONE of the following Risk attitudes can you see being displayed by the Managing Director?

A   Risk seeking

B   Risk cautious

C   Risk averse

D   Risk taker

22 'Risk mapping' is a technique that is commonly used to show risks on a matrix. Which TWO variables form the 'axes' or 'dimensions' of a risk map?

A   Source

B   Category

C   Probability

D   Department

E   Impact

23 The sudden death of the CEO of a small marketing consultancy would best fit which category in a risk map?

A   Low probability; low impact

B   Low probability; high impact

C   High probability; low impact

D   High probability; high impact

24   **X is a large retailer, employing over 20,000 sales staff. The retail industry has a reputation for a high level of staff turnover. The resignation of a member of the sales staff would best fit which category in a risk map?**

A   Low probability; low impact

B   Low probability; high impact

C   High probability; low impact

D   High probability; high impact

25   **The 'TARA' mnemonic is often used to categorise risk management methods. Which one of the following represents the methods in the TARA mnemonic?**

A   Transfer; Assure; Remove; Accept

B   Transfer; Accept; Reduce; Adapt

C   Transfer; Avoid; Reduce; Accept

D   Transfer; Accept; Remove; Adapt

26   **'Net risk' (also known as 'residual risk') is calculated by multiplying probability and impact _____ any action is taken to mitigate the risk.**

Which word correctly completes the sentence above?

A   Before

B   After

27   C Company has recently expanded and now trades in two different countries. Country A is a developed nation with a sophisticated legal system and democratic government.

Country B is a democracy but has a history of corruption and fraud at the highest levels of government.

The board of C Co has noticed that in Country B costs of setting up new premises have been unusually high. On questioning the managers within Country B, the board has learned that 'additional payments' to officials must be made in order to obtain planning permission. In Country A, these kinds of payments would be illegal. Managers in both countries are paid bonuses according to the success of C Co's expansion plans.

The board has decided to prevent these additional payments from being made in the future in order to be able to establish the same ethical standards in both countries. Company C is pursuing an expansion strategy in both countries.

What are the possible risks arising from C Company preventing these payments in future?

Select ALL that apply.

A   Further expansion in Country B will not occur.

B   Expansion in Country A will slow.

C   Staff turnover in Country B will increase.

D   Overall performance of C Company will suffer.

E   C Company's ethical reputation will suffer.

28   Q is a house builder operating in Country P where interest rates are at their lowest point for 20 years. The government of Country P has been encouraging the building of new houses due to a shortage, particularly of 'affordable housing'. Q has taken full advantage of government schemes to help the population purchase new housing and has invested in new machinery, taken on extra staff and begun to build on many of the sites held in its 'land bank'.

Government schemes of particular interest to Q include low interest rate government loans, government backed mortgages and the ability to purchase a share of a home, with the government owning the remaining amount on which rent would be paid according to market rates.

As part of Q's regular risk register review, the possibility of interest rate increases has been flagged.

What are the potential consequences for Q of an increase in interest rates?

Select ALL that apply.

A   Those customers who have purchased houses via government schemes may default on their loans.

B   Q may find demand for its new houses decreases.

C   Q's own costs may increase.

D   The government may withdraw their schemes leading to a drop in demand.

E   The cost of land will increase.

29   J is an organisation which provides veterinary services to large producers of meat and dairy produce in Country P. Lately J has found it difficult to recruit enough qualified veterinarians despite offering excellent terms and conditions. This is partly due to a shortage of newly qualified veterinarians in Country P where training has become very expensive.

J has also had problems sourcing some of the antibiotics and vaccinations it routinely sells to customers for their animals. There is a great deal of controversy surrounding medical intervention into meat and dairy produce and some of J's usual suppliers have had their production disrupted by violent protests. There are many other suppliers of these goods in other countries.

J offers a 24hr support service to its larger customers where it will attend any unexpected emergency or event and offer veterinary services. Recently J was sued by one customer who had used this service when hundreds of cows became suddenly ill on a weekend. Many of the cows died despite J's intervention. Uptake of this 24hr support service is very low since J's customers do not generally feel it is necessary and J is likely to settle the court case soon at great expense.

Directors have also noticed that equipment they issue to staff is getting lost or damaged far more lately and this is adding extra costs to the services they offer. J is unable to increase prices due to the competitive nature of the industry so keeping costs low is very important.

Which of the following would appear to be valid risk management techniques for J?

Select ALL that apply.

A   Transfer the risk of damaged or lost equipment to an insurance company.

B   Reduce the risk of not attracting staff by increasing pay offered significantly.

C   Accept the risk of being unable to source vaccinations and antibiotics.

D   Avoid the risk of further court cases by no longer offering the 24hr support service.

30   **When using the expected value criterion, it is assumed that the individual wants to**

A   maximise return for a given level of risk

B   maximise return irrespective of the level of risk

C   minimise risk for a given level of return

D   minimise risk irrespective of the level of return

31   The following are the forecast purchases of raw materials in a future month:

Forecast purchases for month	Probability of occurrence
£400,000	30%
£500,000	50%
£600,000	20%

Calculate the upside and downside volatility from expected purchases.

32   X is a bank. The management accountant of X has estimated that the value of its asset portfolio at year end will be $1,200 million, with a standard deviation of $430 million.

Calculate the value at risk of the portfolio, at a 95% confidence level.

Express your answer in $, rounded to the nearest million.

$_____

33   F, an internal auditor working for ABC plc, a medium-sized building contractor firm, is concerned with the risk management process with ABC. F has investigated the process at each organisational level extensively and found that, although ABC do identify risks and then respond, the cognitive process involved in analysing the likelihood and impact for each identified risk is not being systematically conducted.

Which ONE of the following steps are missing from ABC's risk management process?

A   Control activities

B   Reporting

C   Risk Assessment

D   Compliance

34   The Committee of Sponsoring Organisations of the Treadway Commission (2003) have developed a three dimensional matrix Enterprise Risk management (ERM) framework

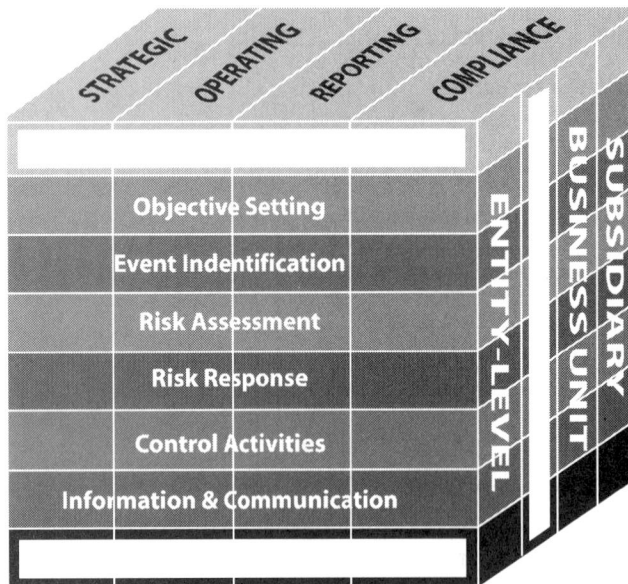

Which THREE are the missing elements of the ERM framework pictured above.

A   Division

B   Monitoring

C   Internal environment

D   PEST

E   core competencies

F   Analysis

35   **The Committee of Sponsoring Organisations (COSO) outlined six key principles of Enterprise Risk Management (ERM). Identify which of the following is/are included.**

Select ALL that apply.

A   Consideration of risk management in the context of business strategy

B   The creation of a risk aware culture

C   Consideration of a narrow range of risks, mainly financial

D   Risk management is the responsibility of the Risk Committee

E   A comprehensive and holistic approach to risk management

36   **X is planning to produce its first 'risk register'. Which of the following aspects of each risk should be included in such a document?**

Select ALL that apply.

A   The probability or likelihood of the risk

B   The name of the risk owner

C   Actions to be taken to mitigate the risk

D   The impact of the risk

E   The level of residual risk associated with the risk

37   **In 1992, the Committee of Sponsoring Organisations (COSO) stated that an effective internal control system consists of five integrated elements. Which of the following are elements of such a system, according to COSO?**

Select ALL that apply.

A   Risk assessment

B   A risk register

C   An internal audit function

D   A control environment

E   Control activities

38   Health plc is a leading innovative pharmaceutical research and manufacturing company with interests across the globe. Yesterday a leading newspaper in a developing country exposed a serious and potentially deadly health risk to employees being exposed to harmful chemicals.

Health plc has not yet reacted to the report and the management are in emergency meetings to decide on the best course of action. Within the meeting the newly appointed Finance Manager remarked on the lack of regard for employees by local managers and a culture of carelessness and neglect.

Which ONE element of the COSO framework for Internal controls is the Finance Manager discussing?

A   Control environment

B   Risk assessment

C   Control activities

D   Monitoring

39   **According to the Financial Reporting Council (FRC) Guidance on Risk Management, Internal Control and Related Financial and Business Reporting, which ONE of the following is ultimately responsible for a company's system of internal controls?**

A   The Financial Controller

B   The Board of Directors

C   The Internal Audit function

D   Every employee

40   The FRC Guidance on Risk Management, Internal Control and Related Financial and Business Reporting stated there are three features of a sound internal control system

Which THREE of the following best describes those three features within the FRC guidance?

A   The principle of Internal control is embedded into the organisation.

B   The board of Director must resign if any internal control failure is found.

C   An organisations' internal control system must be able to respond to changing risks from within and outside the company.

D   An internal auditor must be appointed by every organisation.

E   The internal control system must include a robust and rigorous procedure for reporting.

F   The shareholders must be informed of all internal controls in place in the annual report.

41   X is a retailer of fruit and vegetables. X has recently acquired a number of farm businesses.

Which ONE of the following types of integration is this an example of?

A   Forward Vertical

B   Backward Vertical

C   Horizontal

D   Conglomerate

42   S is a large multinational organisation which operates in many different markets and manufactures many different products. It considers itself to be a conglomerate. The complexity of S's operations has made risk management very difficult in the past since each strategic business unit is so different.

The board of S has recently employed a team of external consultants and asked them to produce and maintain a risk register for S.

The consultants are working on the risk register, which is to be a document with a tabular format and various headings.

Which of the following headings could the board of S expect to see in the risk register produced for S?

Select ALL that apply.

A   Risk Owner

B   Mitigation Actions

C   Overall Risk Ratings

D   Risk Appetite

E   Risk Capacity

43   Global Stores Inc ('GS') is a large multinational retailer famous for its low prices and high value for money. GS has subsidiaries in many different countries and tax jurisdictions and uses transfer pricing to manage its global tax liability. GS and other global companies are coming under increasing criticism in Country E for paying no corporation tax despite revenues exceeding $50 million. Questions have been asked in parliament and the Government of E is now considering changing its tax rules or even imposing a special super tax on prime offenders.

Which ONE of the following is the best response to the criticism?

A   Release a press statement highlighting the fact that GS is doing nothing illegal and, by saving tax, is creating benefits for its shareholders, staff and customers.

B   Ignore the criticism as most customers will be more interested in GS's lower prices than its record on taxation.

C   Make a large donation to a high profile charity in Country E, ensuring it receives maximum publicity as a result.

D   Open discussions with the tax authorities of Country E to negotiate a fairer system of transfer pricing where it pays tax in E without massively increasing global tax liabilities.

44   Having attended a recent conference on the benefits of an ISO accreditation, the Marketing director of YFT plc, an online retailer, has suggested that YFT work towards attaining an ISO accreditation. The Finance director agrees and suggests one relating to risk management. The risk committee have been tasked with making sure the risk treatments that YFT use are appropriate to ISO 31000.

Which ONE of the following risk treatments would NOT be acceptable according to ISO31000?

A   Accepting the risk

B   Sharing the risk

C   Retaining the risk

D   Ignoring the risk

E   Removing the risk source

45   Yulia is a senior manager at a hospital. Currently, eye surgeons perform an average of 3 operations per day and this has left the hospital with a sizeable waiting list for such operations. Yulia wishes to raise this to 5 per day. While she is not offering surgeons a bonus for achieving this new level of performance, she is sure that, as it will benefit patients, they will happily accept the new targets.

Yulia has announced the new targets to her surgeons, who were annoyed as Yulia had not previously consulted them about this issue. Privately, most surgeons have admitted that they could reach 4 operations per day if they hurried through more routine procedures, but are concerned that 5 would adversely impact their primary focus of patient care.

Which ONE of the following problems is Yulia most likely to face with the new targets?

A   Surgeons will see the targets as unachievable and become demotivated by them.

B   Surgeons will rush operations, leading to poorer outcomes for patients and damage to the hospital's reputation.

C   Surgeons will demand that they will only work towards the new targets if they receive bonuses.

D   Surgeons will ignore the targets and do as they have always done.

46   B is a large professional firm of financial advisors which offers bespoke project management services to clients. These services are generally one off in nature and each manager within B is assessed on the successful completion of client projects.

Each project is different and on occasion it is necessary to bring in external expertise to ensure the client gets the specialised service they request. B has an approved list of external consultants which managers can use if they feel it is required.

Over the last quarter, the use of external experts has increased by over 40%, a level the management view as unacceptably high. The profit margin is falling as a result of this and the senior management are concerned that unnecessary costs are being incurred to enable managers to sign off projects quickly.

SUBJECT P3: RISK MANAGEMENT

Which of the following actions might be appropriate to resolve this situation?

Select ALL that apply.

A   Revision of the management reward structure to include use of in house expertise.

B   Negotiation of cheaper outsource rates with external experts.

C   Abolition of the approved list of external consultants.

D   Introduction of a policy whereby senior management must approve all use of external consultants.

E   Monitoring of each project managers use of external experts.

47   Fred is the manager of a toy shop. The shop is part of a large chain of similar retail outlets all selling the company's own brand toys. Fred believes there is a market locally for beach toys since his shop is located by the sea however these kinds of toys are not part of his employers' product range. Fred believes one of the reasons for the underperformance of his shop is the presence of a competitor in the town with a more extensive range of toys including beach toys.

Fred's employer gives him responsibility for staff, premises and all other aspects of the shops day to day running. All other decisions are made centrally. Fred receives a bonus based on the shop's performance. He has not received his bonus due to the poor performance of the shop for three consecutive years.

Which of the following performance measures are likely to demotivate Fred if his bonus is based on them?

Select ALL that apply.

A   Revenue growth.

B   Growth in net profit.

C   Control of overheads.

D   Return on investment.

E   Staff turnover.

F   Customer satisfaction.

48   Goggle plc is a multi-national software company. They have a head office in London and further large offices on each continent. They employ over 20,000 staff. It is a modern company with forward-thinking directors who believe that if staff are happy Goggle will receive their best work.

Goggle has installed non-work areas and activities at each office to keep its staff happy. For example, each major office has a 'play area' where there is a gym, table tennis, pool tables, a small crazy golf course and the like, which staff may access at any time subject to performing their work duties.

The average cost of one play area has been around £1 million.

Which of the following are possible non-financial benefits at Goggle?

Select ALL that apply.

A   Increased productivity

B   Increased efficiency

C   Increased expenditure

D   Increased staff satisfaction

49 LAP is an external training organisation. LAP teach trainee computer programmers' basic skills early in their career – usually in the first few weeks of gaining employment, and usually for the next three years of their careers. The trainees are awarded a Diploma by LAP which is highly prized and often ensures a well-paid job in the future.

Tutors at LAP work in one of 12 offices around the UK – all in large cities. LAP cannot employ enough tutors with the correct skills mainly due to the salary being offered – it is insufficient ($150 per day) compared to the salary which could be earned outside of LAP. (LAP tutors also receive a pension, holiday pay, travel expenses, etc.) Staff at LAP are utilised only 65% of the time but their skills vary and any one tutor cannot teach all courses.

LAP often employ freelancers to cover any gaps and pay them in excess of a full-time LAP employee. This is well-known amongst LAP staff, and the braver ones have left LAP to return on a freelance basis, increasing their earnings considerably (a fixed fee of $300 per day).

Where possible LAP move staff across offices to cover any courses that do not have a tutor. There is a recharge of $350 per day from one office to another.

Which of the following should LAP do to become more cost efficient?

Select ALL that apply.

A   Employ more skilled full-time staff on a higher salary.

B   Offer current staff overtime.

C   Always use full-time staff from other offices before freelancers.

D   Only use freelancers.

50 EV Ltd is a medium sized company specialising in storage, providing flexible, secure and affordable storage solutions in the country of Hoardland. EV Ltd has a property portfolio of over 100 storage facilities located throughout the country.

As part of the risk management process, EV Ltd ask an external consultant to assess the security of each of the storage locations. EV Ltd is interested in all the potential physical access points and how likely a security breach is perceived to be. Each location has, as much as is possible, the same security features and so in theory the likelihood of a security breach is the same for each property in their portfolio.

The external consultant has identified that that there are two ways in which the storage locations could be broken into. They are on opposite sides of the buildings and because of the size of the buildings it is unlikely that someone would attempt to attack both in one night, it would either be an attack at the front of the building, or an attack at the back of the building. The front of the building includes the main entrance and is considered the most likely access point. Knowledge of the access points at the rear of the building is less well known and so is perceived to be less likely.

As a result of this, there is more security at the front of the building to help mitigate this higher likelihood. If someone were to attack the front of the building they would have to get past a motion sensor detection system, a secure locked door and avoid being seen on CCTV which is observed by an onsite security guard. The external consultant has estimated the likelihood of breaching these controls as 5%, 10% and 15% respectively. At the rear, there is no motion sensor, just one securely locked door and CCTV, the consultant estimates the likelihood of attack here as 10% and 15%.

Considering the controls in place, which of the following statements are correct?

Select ALL that apply.

A   The overall probability of a successful break in is 9%

B   The overall probability of a successful break in is 1.575%

C   There is a higher probability of a successful break in at the rear

D   There is a higher probability of a successful break in at the front

E   The probability of a successful break in at the rear is 7.5%.

F   The probability of a successful break in at the front is 0.075%.

STRATEGIC RISK

51   The board of PLK Company is meeting to discuss the future of the company. The company has always used a formal long-term planning approach to developing its future strategy.

Which of the following factors will increase the risks associated with using this planning approach?

Select ALL that apply.

A   Existing bank loans are due to be renegotiated

B   Recent expansion has led to the promotion of inexperienced managers

C   The board us under pressure from investors to ensure a dividend is paid this year

D   PLK pursues a cost leadership strategy

E   PLK operates in a fast-changing competitive industry

52   GUY Company manufactures high-fashion clothes in G-Land. The company's main markets are retail outlets in countries overseas. GUY works to exploit economies of scale to keep its prices competitively low.

Which one of the following factors would be MOST likely to increase the risks associated with this strategy?

A   A change in the market leading to demand for high-fashion clothes becoming more elastic

B   The currency of G-Land strengthens against that of its main overseas markets

C   Costs of advertising and marketing increase

D   Investors become more keenly focused on GUY's return on capital employed

53   BVG Company is a manufacturer making expensive highly branded products for sale to a small but loyal customer base.

Its production process requires consistently high-quality supplies of one key raw material – the T – so BVG is considering expanding into production of Ts to secure its supply chain.

The current market in T production is highly competitive and close attention to cost control and the exploitation of economies of scale to maintain low prices is seen as a vital component of success.

During a board meeting to discuss the proposals, a number of conflicting views were expressed.

Based on the information provided, which of the following statements concerning the expansion proposal are TRUE?

Select ALL that apply.

A   The expansion proposal does not appear to fit with BVG Company's current generic strategy

B   The proposal is the logical extension of BVG's resource-based approach to strategic planning

C   Organic growth would allow BVG to avoid the existing barriers to entry in the T production industry

D   Since existing T producers are not listed companies, a due diligence appraisal will not be required in the case of acquisition

E   To minimise competitor reaction, acquiring an existing T-supplier would be better than attempting organic growth

54   POZ Company is developing a range of new products. It hopes that one of its products will be able to open up a new market and significantly disrupt several existing ones.

Which TWO of the following factors are MOST likely to enhance the success of POZs attempts to disrupt the market with a new product?

A   The product will require users to complete an on-line training course to understand its features

B   The product could be quickly distributed to a wide range of customers

C   Significant amounts have been spent on product research and development

D   The product is compatible with items already owned by much of the target population

E   The product improves the quality of an existing item in the market

55   HGJ Company is a home entertainment retailer operating through a chain of stores. Despite the development of many other forms of personal technology, such as computers, the chain has deliberately limited its reach to home entertainment. Although shareholders are kept satisfied with annual dividends the company has always argued that employee satisfaction is its main priority claiming that enthusiastic staff make more sales. It has a balanced scorecard approach to performance measurement with store managers required to focus on nine key metrics under each perspective. Stores in the chain compete to make the highest sales figures each week, with employees within the winning store sharing the resulting bonus.

The board of HGJ have been advised to conduct a stress test assessment of the company's business operations.

Which of the following strategic decisions would a stress testing assessment be MOST likely to challenge?

A   Limiting products to home entertainment

B   Prioritising staff over shareholders

C   Developing extensive scorecard metrics

D   Encouraging stores to compete with each other

56 HGT hospital has come under increasing pressure to improve its performance and in particular to improve efficiency.

As a result several new strategies have been put forward.

Which TWO of the following strategies are focused on improving efficiency?

A Centralising purchasing to reduce overall spending on sterile supplies

B Introducing activity based costing to drive down ward costs per patient

C Increasing spending on post-operative care to improve patient outcomes

D Streamlining booking processes to reduce waiting lists

E Redesigning ward layouts to increase overall daily bed occupancy rates

57 GST Company is reviewing its raw material supply chain. Although the risk of a breakdown in the supply chain is not believed to be likely, the short term impact of such a breakdown could be highly damaging for its business.

The board has decided to undertake scenario planning to help it mitigate the impact of such an event should it arise.

Which ONE of the following statements describes the use of scenario planning to mitigate the impact of a breakdown in GST's supply chain?

A Identification of factors which might give rise to a breakdown in supply and development of a series of potential responses to enact in the event it occurs

B Evaluation a range of potential strategies to prevent a breakdown and implementation of the optimal one

C A review GST's priorities and its ability to be flexible and productive and identification of its critical performance variables and constraints

D Consideration of the actions of GST's competitors in the event of a supply breakdown and formulation of a response based on their likely response

58 BJK Company is a family owned company with a preference for operating independently. The company has designed a new product and market research suggests sales of the product could be much higher than first imagined. The board has agreed that it will not therefore be possible for BJK to manufacture and distribute the product on its own and a meeting has been scheduled to discuss the available options.

It is more important for BJK to earn profits from the product design than to dictate how the product is marketed and sold.

Based on the information provided, which ONE of the following methods of joint development would be MOST appropriate for BJK Company to use to exploit their new product?

A Licensing

B Franchising

C Joint venture

D Strategic alliance

59   BHG Company is a small family company with a small tight-knit employee team and a known reputation for product quality and excellent customer service.   Budgets are tightly controlled to ensure that all financial obligations can be met, and the board has a preference for developing strategy gradually by building on previously tried and tested policies.   The company's existing strategy, to expand its customer base by growing its sales force, was agreed a year ago and is currently being implemented.

Owing to economic and political market fluctuations, the company is facing an uncertain future and the board is meeting to determine the most appropriate response.

Based on the information provided, which ONE of the following techniques would be MOST suitable for the company to adopt?

A   Undertake scenario planning

B   Determine a generic competitive strategy

C   Stress test current strategy

D   Develop disruptive innovation

60   FHY Company is an established manufacturer of high-tech products with strong cash reserves. It has a well regarded brand and its products regularly come top of consumer rankings for reliability and value for money. However in recent years, newer competitors have begun to enter the market, offering products that offer customers many more features and greater flexibility. FHY's sales have therefore begun to fall sharply. The board of FHY believe that the company should build on its reputation for excellence and has responded by increasing spending on research and development in order to update its own product range.

Which ONE of the following factors currently affecting FHY will be MOST likely to increase the risks associated with this approach to strategic planning?

A   The market for FHY's products is changing rapidly

B   FHY's shareholders are expecting a payment of a dividend this year

C   FHY's customers place a high value on simplicity of the user experience

D   Some manufacturers are concentrating on delivering more basic products at a far lower cost

61   The board at BGF Company has been monitoring the falling share price of its main competitor after a large-scale accounting fraud there was uncovered by auditors.

BGF's board are keen to avoid a similar situation arising within BGF and plan to implement a number of changes aimed at minimising the opportunity for fraud to occur.

Which ONE of the following actions is MOST likely to minimise the opportunity for fraud within BGF?

A   Strengthening the company's internal control environment

B   Paying employees a fair wage

C   Setting up a fraud reporting system

D   Monitoring employees vacation balances

62 FUO Company manufactures high fashion garments. One of its fabric suppliers is currently under investigation for poor employment practices and in light of the current news coverage, FUO's board wishes to preserve its reputation as an ethical fashion chain.

Which ONE of the following actions would be MOST likely to help preserve FUO's reputation?

A   Prevent employees from discussing details of FUO's supply chain

B   Provide full disclosure of the companies in FUO's supply chain

C   Incorporate a commitment to ensuring an ethical supply chain into its advertising message

D   Provide board members with training to deflect media queries

63 BHY Company wishes to improve the company's reputation.

The chief executive believes that the company should adopt a policy of corporate social responsibility (CSR), with a particular focus on environmental issues, to underpin the development of future corporate strategies.

However, several of the other board members have expressed reservations about the implications of introducing such a policy.

Which of the following statements made by BHY's board members are true?

Select ALL that apply.

A   CSR means prioritising the needs of external stakeholders over those of shareholders

B   BHY will need to develop additional metrics to measure the results of the CSR policy

C   Adopting a CSR policy will cause costs to rise

D   Developing a CSR policy will require an understanding of society's values

E   A CSR approach would help BHY to anticipate future environmental legislation

64 BJI Company has discovered that one of its products, launched into the market with considerable fanfare a few months ago, has a design fault which can lie latent for a considerable period before suddenly causing the product to become unusable. BJI's design team believe it is unlikely that the fault would ever be spotted by consumers – even if their product did stop working.

Which of the following risk management strategies would be MOST likely to minimise the potential reputational damage associated with the fault?

A   Take no action unless the fault is discovered in which case recall the affected products

B   Recall the affected products now without explanation

C   Go public about the fault now and recall the affected products

D   Take no action and deny the existence of a fault if necessary

65 The industry regulator for SRT Company has ruled that several of its products contravene existing health and safety regulations.

The board of SRT is meeting to discuss its response.

Which of the following stakeholders should the company consider when attempting to minimise the reputational damage resulting from the regulator's finding?

Select ALL that apply.

A   Shareholders

B   Customers

C   Staff

D   Suppliers

E   Investors

66 BHP group is an international company which has always worked to minimise its overall tax liability. Recently after a spate of negative publicity, several of the members of the board of BHP were replaced.

BHPs manufacturing company (MD) makes caravans in Country A where its group head office is also based. County A has a low corporation tax rate. The caravans are then shipped to Country B where the group has two companies: new and second-hand caravan sales outlets (SO) and caravan repair and servicing centres (RSC). Country B has a high corporation tax rate.

Customers buying a new caravan can offer their existing caravan in part exchange. These existing caravans are then transferred to RSCs to be refurbished. RSCs are paid by group head office on a direct-cost-plus basis.

Sales managers at SOs receive bonuses for new caravan sales based on the listed purchase price (regardless of the amount paid for existing caravans in part exchange). Bonuses on used caravan sales are based on the actual sales price (exchange value less the cost of refurbishment).

The newly appointed board at BHP group is concerned that this business model may be incentivising behaviour which could have further negative repercussions for its reputation.

Based on the information provided, which of the following statements regarding the potential impact of this business model are TRUE?

Select ALL that apply.

A   Sales staff at the SOs will be incentivised to offer a high part exchange value for the old caravans

B   BHP will want MD to transfer caravans to SO at the lowest possible transfer price

C   BHP will wish to pay the lowest possible price for the refurbishment work performed by RSC

D   SO will benefit if costs are minimised in RSC

E   RSC is incentivised to minimise costs

67   The board of UPL Company wishes to put in place a series of performance measures to monitor its reputation. One area of interest is the reputation of the company's products in the wider market place.

Which THREE of the following performance measures would be MOST likely to help UPL to monitor the reputation of its products?

A   Fluctuation of the company share price

B   Number of product returns

C   Employee turnover

D   Customer interviews

E   Analysis of on-line consumer review forums

68   The board of BVC Company is meeting to discuss its reputational risk.

The media director wishes to introduce a reputation risk management system rather than relying on the crisis management system already in place.

Which THREE of the following features apply to reputation risk management systems?

A   Driven by media and other uncontrollable events

B   Based on assessment of issues likely to impact the company

C   Part of long-term planning process

D   Require regular updates and tests of response plans

E   Built into corporate culture

69   PLU group has been criticised in the media for the way in which it prices transfers between group companies based in different countries. This criticism has negatively affected its reputation.

Which of the following objectives of transfer pricing is MOST likely to give rise to media criticism?

A   Minimisation of group global tax liability

B   Maintenance of goal congruence across the group

C   Provision of corporate autonomy

D   Recording movement of goods and services between companies

70   **Which of the following statements about corporate social responsibility (CSR) are TRUE?**

Select ALL that apply.

A   CSR is another name for brand management

B   Only companies with publicly traded shares need to report to stakeholders on their CSR work

C   CSR requires engagement of the senior leadership team

D   CSR can lower the costs of doing business

E   CSR decisions affect investor relations

71 X uses cost leadership to help provide a competitive advantage, the board have met recently as they are concerned about risks to its corporate reputation.

Which of the following risks directly affect the reputation of X?

Select ALL that apply.

A   A key supplier of X is based in a 'low wage economy', and is known by X to employ staff as young as 8 years of age.

B   The packaging used by X is not recyclable, and contains small traces of a known toxin.

C   X delivers its products by road and air.

D   X pays staff at levels below the average for its industry.

E   X does business with several non-democratic or repressive governments.

72 MLC is a clothing retailer who imports clothes from diverse suppliers worldwide. MLC has a very strong, well publicised corporate ethical code. The company accountant has just found out that one of MLC suppliers use child labour in the manufacture of their clothes and pay very low wages with cramped, dangerous conditions. This is in breach of contract conditions with that supplier.

Which ONE of the following statements best describes the actions MLC should take in the light of this?

A   Place more orders with the supplier – it's cheap labour so the margins are good, which should keep the shareholders happy.

B   Leave things as they are and hope the information doesn't get out.

C   Continue trading with the supplier but investigate the claims quietly.

D   Cancel all contracts with the supplier and release a press statement stating how the company will always act quickly and decisively if unethical practices are suspected.

73 DMI operates a chain of ice cream parlours and pizza takeaways in a local seaside area. They have three outlets in the area and have won awards for their ice cream flavours. On sunny days there are often queues outside. The chain is owned in a partnership between two family members, Carlota and Aurora.

Carlota has become increasingly concerned about reputation risk and has recently been reading some articles about reputation risk. At the next meeting between the two owners, Carlota raises the issue and a discussion follows.

Which of the following statements made by the two owners about reputation are correct?

Select ALL that apply.

A   Reputation is something that the organisation can control, to a certain extent. It's about what the organisation does and how it approaches its products, services and actions.

B   A newspaper article highlighting how much waste had been collected by a local school on a beach clean featured several DMI ice cream tubs and pizza boxes. This could have a negative impact on the local reputation of DMI.

C   Reputation risk is rarely related to other forms of risk.

D   Reputation risk can be both an upside risk and a downside risk.

E   Reputation is what people think and communicate about an organisation, it is much harder to control than a brand.

74 You are a management accountant working at a UK listed chemical company. During the course of your duties, you become aware that the company is dumping waste illegally. You have raised this with your manager who has told you to ignore the issue.

Which ONE of the following is NOT an appropriate course of action to take next?

A   Contacting CIMA's ethical helpline for advice

B   Reporting the company to the environment agency

C   Contacting a journalist at a national newspaper

D   Taking the matter to the Audit committee

75 **Which THREE of the following are common arguments FOR organisations adopting a strong approach to corporate social responsibility (CSR)?**

A   Increased profitability due to cost reductions

B   Faster strategic decision-making

C   Improved reputation with environmentally conscious customers

D   Ability to attract higher calibre staff

E   Reduced risk of government intervention in the future

76 HH is a fashion retailer, selling women's clothing in developed countries. HH's customers expect prices to be kept very low and since the market is so competitive, these customers can easily switch to HH's rivals if they do not like the styles or prices on offer in HH's chain of 300 shops.

HH sources garments from many different suppliers but recently the board has learnt that one of its main suppliers has been using child labour in the manufacture of HH's products. Child labour is not illegal in the developing country this supplier operates in and is culturally acceptable there.

HH is aware that child labour is not acceptable in the developed countries where it sells its products. Continued use of the supplier in question is likely to lead to international media coverage and this could subsequently lead to significant damage to HH's reputation.

However, HH has committed to purchase hundreds of new designs from the supplier and if they are no longer able to deal with them, in the short term inventory will be low and customers will be lost.

The board of B have decided to ignore the use of child labour at the supplier for now and deal with media coverage and response as and when it occurs. A plan to introduce minimum standards for suppliers will be unveiled when media coverage occurs and should help manage any controversy.

Which of the following are likely risks resulting from this course of action?

Select ALL that apply.

A   Risk that the company's clothing sales fall if media coverage occurs sooner than expected.

B   Risk that HH cannot source an alternative supplier if necessary.

C   Risk that HH's costs increase.

D   Risk that the company's decision to wait and see becomes public and the company is seen as unethical.

77 CIMA's Code of Ethics contains five fundamental principles of professional ethics for management accountants.

Which of the following are fundamental principles, according to the Code?

Select ALL that apply.

A   Confidentiality

B   Honesty

C   Objectivity

D   Respect

E   Integrity

78 **Which THREE of the following are valid reasons for disclosing commercially sensitive information to a third party which would NOT breach the ethical principle of confidentiality?**

A   It is required due to a professional, ethical dilemma

B   It is permitted by law and authorised by the client

C   It is required by law

D   Failure to disclose could materially disadvantage the third party

E   There is a professional duty or right to disclose the information

79 Ximena is a CIMA® member, and advises a range of individual clients and organisations. Ximena has been asked by a client to write to one of the client's customers, threatening to report them to the tax authorities if they do not pay a debt due to Ximena's client.

To do this would be in breach of which ONE of the fundamental ethical principles (according to CIMA's Code of Ethics)?

A   integrity

B   objectivity

C   professional competence and due care

D   confidentiality

E   professional behaviour

80 Georgi is a CIMA® member, and advises a range of individual clients and organisations. Georgi has been asked, by his sister, to prepare her tax return. Georgi's sister has offered to share any reduction in tax, compared to what she paid last year.

To do this would be in breach of which ONE of the fundamental ethical principles (according to CIMA's Code of Ethics)?

A   integrity

B   objectivity

C   professional competence and due care

D   confidentiality

E   professional behaviour

81   Peter is a CIMA® member, and advises a range of individual clients and organisations. Peter has not carried out any Continuing Professional Development (CPD) activity for five years.

This is in breach of which ONE of the fundamental ethical principles (according to CIMA's Code of Ethics)?

A   integrity

B   objectivity

C   professional competence and due care

D   confidentiality

E   professional behaviour

82   Gregor is a CIMA® member, and advises a range of individual clients and organisations. Gregor has been asked, by a prospective new client, to divulge details of another client's business activities.

To do this would be in breach of which ONE of the fundamental ethical principles (according to CIMA's Code of Ethics)?

A   integrity

B   objectivity

C   professional competence and due care

D   confidentiality

E   professional behaviour

83   CIMA's Code of Ethics recommends a four-step process to resolve any ethical conflict.

What is the correct sequence for those steps?

Refuse to remain associated with the conflict	
Check the facts	
Escalate externally	
Escalate internally	

84   John is a CIMA® member, working as Financial Controller of a listed public company. John has shares in the company, and knows that the share price depends to some extent on the reported profits. John is responsible for producing the published accounts of the company.

According to CIMA's Code of Ethics, which ONE of the following types of ethical threat does this represent?

A   self interest

B   self review

C   advocacy

D   intimidation

E   familiarity

85 Gemma is a CIMA® member, working as Financial Controller of a listed public company.

The company is in the process of applying for additional loan finance. Gemma has been asked to write to the company's bank, providing a forecast of future cash flows which she knows to be very optimistic.

According to CIMA's Code of Ethics, which ONE of the following types of ethical threat does this represent?

A   self interest

B   self review

C   advocacy

D   intimidation

E   familiarity

86 Stephanie has worked in the finance department of Alpha for 5 years and has been promoted to work alongside the management accountant. Stephanie is currently working towards CIMA's CGMA® qualification.

The CGMA® qualified finance professional working as a management accountant of Alpha, has told Stephanie that they will be working closely with department heads to produce their annual budgets. The management accountant is happy to allow significant 'slack' to be built in to these budgets to make them easier to achieve since, in their opinion, this makes Alpha a much more relaxed place to work.

Following this conversation, Stephanie overheard the management accountant agreeing to alter budgeted production figures to make them easier to achieve in return for tickets to a major event. When she questioned her manager, she received a response stating no harm was done since the budgeted figures are subjective anyway.

Which of the following ethical principles is the management accountant in breach of?

Select ALL that apply.

A   Integrity.

B   Objectivity.

C   Professional competence and due care.

D   Confidentiality.

E   Professional Behaviour.

87 Travel Co is a travel company. Its head office is in Germany but it operates throughout Europe. It is a multi-million dollar business with thousands of employees at head office, in high-street branches throughout Europe, and within the hotels it sends customers to.

Travel Co has been in the world news recently due to a tragic event which occurred six years ago at one of the hotels it contracts with. Two people died in their hotel room due to a faulty boiler giving off poisonous carbon monoxide fumes while they slept.

The other family members have spent the past six years fighting for compensation from TC. The court case heard how Travel Co contracted for rooms in the hotel. Part of the contract stated that the rooms should be 'safe' for their customers. The hotel manager signed the agreement but made no effort to check each room for its safety.

The family's contract was with Travel Co. Travel Co's contract was with the hotel. The court case has now been decided and Travel Co has been awarded $3 million in compensation. The hotel had broken its contract by not making the rooms safe. The family were awarded nothing by the court since their contract was with Travel Co, who had done nothing contractually wrong.

Travel Co's Board has since decided to give the family $350,000 as a gesture of goodwill. Travel Co's actions have been criticised in the national press and on international television. TV coverage is showing families packing carbon monoxide detectors in their suitcases prior to travelling to Europe. Interviews with other families have covered their disgust at Travel Co's actions. No apology has ever been given by Travel Co.

Travel Co's share price has fallen by 10% over the past week.

This morning Travel Co's Board announced their profits for the year and their CEO is to be awarded an $11 million bonus.

Which THREE of the following courses of action are most appropriate for Travel Co?

A   Travel Co should issue an apology to the family.

B   Travel Co should award the full $3 million to the family.

C   Travel Co should abide by the ruling of the court case.

D   Travel Co should investigate every hotel room for safety.

E   Travel Co should be pleased that the court case has raised the awareness of the Travel Co brand.

88   Catalina is a CGMA® qualified finance professional. She decided to leave her job as a management accountant at XYZ plc to start her own business. As a dog lover she opened a dog grooming salon in a town near to her home. She rented premises, just off the high street and near the local park, from the local council. The rent was advertised as $4,500 per annum but, due to the dilapidated state of the premises, she managed to negotiate a discount and paid only $350 per month. The council required one months' rent to be paid up front in lieu of a bond.

Catalina employed two members of staff – one a qualified groomer, and one as a trainee groomer. The trainee groomer attended college on day per week, leaving the groomer to work alone that day. Catalina managed the bookings, the bank account, wages, advertising and inventory.

The business quickly established itself and word spread in the local area that the service provided was good. Many customers returned every six to eight weeks, happy with the service. However, the local area didn't appear to have sufficient dogs to maximise capacity, so Catalina had to terminate the trainee's employment contract (within her three-month probation period). The disgruntled trainee did not receive the news of losing her job well and decided to take revenge by discrediting the business. Having copied the client details of some of the salons best customers she telephoned them at home and told them of terrible things that were done to their beloved pets while at the salon. These events were not true.

By the end of the first nine months it became apparent that the business would do well for one individual i.e. the groomer (whose wages were fixed) but there was insufficient profit left over for Catalina to take a salary. Catalina decided to sell the business, which the groomer was more than happy to buy. The agreed purchase price was $5,000. This was paid immediately.

The rental agreement between Catalina and the council continued until the year end. Catalina still had to pretend that she was the business owner or she would be in breach of contract – one of the contract terms was that there was to be no sub-letting. On two occasions when the council telephoned Catalina's home telephone number she pretended that she still ran the business. The groomer agreed with the charade.

Catalina continued to pay the rent to the council each month until the contract end, the groomer having paid Catalina first.

Catalina paid the rent by debit card over the telephone. One month, towards the end of the rental contract, the council misallocated the rent received by them and allocated it in error to their rates department. The grooming business was rates exempt so the rates department returned the $350 to Catalina.

At the end of the year, after receiving the bond back, Catalina immediately closed the grooming business bank account and changed her telephone number. The council have not been in touch about the 'missing' months' rent yet.

Which THREE of the following ethical principles has Catalina and her staff NOT met?

A   Integrity

B   Objectivity

C   Confidentiality

D   Professional behaviour

E   Professional competence and due care

89   **Which ONE of the following is NOT a benefit of corporate governance?**

A   Improved access to capital markets

B   Stimulation of performance

C   Enhanced marketability of goods and services

D   Prevention of fraudulent claims by contractors

90   **The 'agency problem' refers to which ONE of the following situations?**

A   Shareholders acting in their own short-term interests rather than the long-term interests of the company.

B   A vocal minority of shareholders expecting the directors to act as their agents and pay substantial dividends.

C   Companies reliant upon substantial government contracts such that they are effectively agents of the government.

D   The directors acting in their own interests rather than the shareholders' interests.

91 **Which TWO of the following are functions of audit committees?**

1   Planning the annual external audit.

2   Reviewing the effectiveness of internal financial controls.

3   Reviewing and monitoring the external auditor's independence.

4   Processing year end journal adjustments to the financial statements.

A   1 and 2

B   1 and 3

C   2 and 4

D   2 and 3

92 **Which ONE of the following is the main reason for the roles of the chair and chief executive to be held by different people?**

A   To ensure that there is more than one person overseeing the organisation.

B   To ensure decision making power is not concentrated in the hands of one individual.

C   To ensure the CEO can manage staff whilst the chair meets potential investors.

93 The UK Corporate Governance regime recommends that large listed companies should form an Audit Committee consisting of independent non-executive directors.

The Audit Committee should be responsible for which of the following?

Select ALL that apply.

A   Carrying out internal audit activities

B   Managing internal audit activities

C   Recommending appointment, or removal of the company's external auditor

D   Reviewing the company's system of internal financial controls

E   Carrying out external audit activities

94 The UK Corporate Governance regime recommends that large listed companies should form a Remuneration Committee.

The Remuneration Committee should be responsible for which of the following?

Select ALL that apply.

A   Setting the remuneration level of the Executive Directors

B   Setting the remuneration level of the chair

C   Recommending on the remuneration level of the Senior Managers

D   Setting the remuneration level of the Non-Executive Directors

E   Setting the remuneration level of the External Auditor

95   The remuneration committee of Ghee plc, a listed company, consists of 4 Directors with the HR Director chairing the committee. The other three members are NED's although only one of these has been assessed as independent by the nominations committee. The remuneration committee has responsibility for both executive and non-executive pay policy with these policies being put forward by approval at the AGM by shareholders.

What actions should Ghee take to comply with best practice corporate governance?

Select ALL that apply.

A   HR Director should resign from Ghee

B   HR director should resign from the chair position of the remuneration committee

C   Non-independent NED should resign from the remuneration committee

D   Remuneration committee should not have responsibility for NED remuneration

E   All NEDs on remuneration committee should be replaced

96   Monk plc, a listed entity, currently has a governance structure that consists of an Executive chair, who acts as both chair and CEO, together with 4 executive directors and 1 non-executive director.

Which ONE of the following would you recommend in order for Monk plc to comply with best practice corporate governance?

A   Removing the non-executive director as he/she/they will most likely have little knowledge of the business due to a lack of day to day involvement.

B   Creating a separate role for chair and CEO to replace the current role of Executive chair, recruiting an independent person for the position of chair and recruiting additional non-executive directors to create a more balanced board.

C   Replacing the role of Executive chair with the post of CEO and recruiting additional non-executive directors to create a more balanced board.

97   **Which ONE of the following does NOT represent good corporate governance?**

A   Membership of the audit committee should include at least three non-executive directors.

B   Ensuring that non-executive directors do not participate at board meetings.

C   Segregation between the roles of chair and chief executive officer.

D   At least one member of the audit committee should have recent, relevant financial experience.

98   **Which ONE of the following remuneration package elements for Directors will best ensure goal congruence between the interests of shareholders and executive directors?**

A   Cash bonus paid to directors if the company achieves profit growth targets.

B   Cash bonus paid if directors achieve a range of individual performance related targets linked to the balanced scorecard.

C   Share option bonus scheme that is paid if the company achieves profit growth targets.

D   Private Health insurance for directors and their immediate family.

99 YY is a large listed company which makes soft drinks. The company has just experienced a very volatile 3 year period. During this time, the additive used to sweeten YY's products was made illegal in many of its core markets. In addition, the CEO and chair both resigned and the finance director was removed following a conviction for insider training.

The new CEO has a strong manufacturing background but no direct experience of the soft drinks industry. At the next board meeting the CEO wishes to discuss the role of NED's in supporting him/her/them given this lack of expertise. In his/her/their opinion, the NED's main function is to ensure the strategies of YY are realistic and achievable.

The company has 4 NED's, 2 of whom held senior positions in the soft drinks industry before their retirement from full time work. All four NED's have been in post for over 5 years.

Which of the following roles should the CEO expect the NED's to carry out in order to support him?

Select ALL that apply.

A   The setting of new strategies for YY.

B   The scrutiny of strategies already proposed by the board.

C   The monitoring of strategies for excessive risk.

D   The analysis of the external environment.

E   The recruitment of a new Finance Director.

100 According to a recent analyst's report, F is the only company out of the 150 biggest in Geeland which still has a unified chief executive-chair.

Over the last year, several key investors have expressed concern that this is the case and urged the board of F to consider splitting the roles. In their opinion, an independent chair of the board of directors would eliminate the structural conflict of interest caused by the chief executive being his/her/their own boss, and would clarify where the authority of the chief executive ends and responsibility of the board begins.

The board of F are however happy with the current situation and have no plans to change.

Which of the following are likely arguments to maintain a unified chair and chief executive role at F?

Select ALL that apply.

A   The board has appointed a senior independent director with the authority to act as though he/she/they were the non-executive chair when required.

B   Chairing the board in a large institution is a heavy workload and the pressures and breadth of responsibility borne by the chief executive are now almost beyond the capacity of a single person.

C   There are many examples of corporate failure where the roles of chief executive and chair were split.

D   A combined CEO and chair role will command a much higher level of remuneration than a single role of CEO.

E   A board led by an independent chair is more likely to identify and monitor areas of the company that are drifting from its mandate and to put into place corrective measures to get it back on track.

101 The board of Bax Miking Plc have recently decided to appoint some new members to the board. The marketing director, Moussa, has put his daughter forward. His daughter, Zahra, is 23 and has just completed studying towards a financial qualification in her first full time job. He feels that she would be a great addition to the board and would be able to join both the audit committee, and the remuneration committee.

Which of the following statements are true?

Select ALL that apply.

A   Zahra could be an independent non-executive director for Bax Miking Plc.

B   Zahra's financial expertise would make her an ideal candidate for the audit committee.

C   Zahra should not be on the audit committee.

D   It would not be good corporate governance to have Zahra on the remuneration committee.

E   Zahra is unlikely to have enough experience.

F   Zahra would need to have worked at Bax Miking for 5 years before she could become a director.

G   Zahra needs to have more qualifications before she would be able to work on the board at Max Biking Plc.

INTERNAL CONTROLS

102 Controls can be classified into three broad categories: Financial, non-financial quantitative (quantitative) and non-financial qualitative (qualitative).

Match the examples below to the appropriate category.

Category
Financial
Quantitative
Qualitative

Example
Employee training
Customer satisfaction score
Variance analysis
Reviewing aged debt listing
Organisational structure
Absenteeism rate

103 Controls can be classified into three broad categories: Financial, non-financial quantitative (quantitative) and non-financial qualitative (qualitative).

Match the examples below to the appropriate category.

Category
Financial
Quantitative
Qualitative

Example
Number of defects
Lock on a store room door
Bank reconciliations
Contract of employment
Budgetary controls
Number of new products launched

104 In 2013 COSO updated their model of internal control to include 17 principles. 9 of the principles related to the components of 'control environment' and 'risk assessment'.

Drag and drop the following principles into the correct component.

	Control environment	Risk assessment
Clear objectives to allow risk identification and assessment		
That risk identification and analysis does take place across the entity		
The potential for fraud arising in pursuit of the stated objectives must be considered		
The organisation shows a commitment to ethical values		
Accountability of employees for their areas of responsibility		
Human resource policies and practices to help attract, develop and retain suitable talent		
The internal controls system must be reviewed for changes in the external environment		

105 DF plc has identified a critical success factor (CSF) for its organisation:

'Having an excellent quality product.'

Which ONE of the following would be the most suitable control measure to use to help maintain this CSF?

A   Reduce the number of defects identified by quality control and customers by 15%.

B   Reduce the average time taken to deal with complaints about quality by 10%.

C   Increase quality by 50% over the next year.

D   Increase the amount of quality training for production staff.

106 Steve is a recently qualified Management Accountant who has just started working at Bobbles Ltd, a small building firm based in the UK.

One of Steve's duties is to oversee the internal controls of the company. However Steve is not sure how far his remit extends, as he is unsure what is covered by the term 'internal controls'.

Which ONE of the following would best describe the broad term of internal controls?

A   A financial restriction place on the company.

B   An activity, which has been ordered to be completed by the auditors of a company.

C   An activity, which is in place to control certain risks and to help an organisation achieve its objectives.

D   An activity the human resources department conducts to ensure all employees are doing their job correctly.

107 SSS plc is a supermarket based in the UK and another European country. SSS's internal auditor has identified the following risks and internal controls to reduce those risks

Reconcile the FOUR risks to the FOUR internal controls.

Internal Controls		Risks	
A	Prepare and reconcile budget to actual spend	1	The risk of overspending on a construction project
B	Hedging techniques	2	The risk of employees stealing products
C	Tight stock control systems	3	The risk of obsolescence, due to items with a short period of consumption
D	CCTV cameras in store	4	The risk of exchange rate fluctuation between Stirling and the Euro.

108 Which TWO of the following are objectives of the controls in the revenue cycle?

1 Goods are only supplied to customers who pay promptly and in full

2 All purchases are made with reliable and competitively priced suppliers

3 Orders are despatched promptly and in full to the correct customer

4 Only genuine employees are paid

A 1 and 2

B 1 and 3

C 2 and 3

D 3 and 4

109 Which TWO of the following are objectives of the controls in the payroll cycle?

1 Expenditure is recorded accurately and related payables are recorded at an appropriate value.

2 All purchases and related payables are recorded.

3 Correct amounts owed are recorded and paid to the taxation authorities.

4 Employees are paid at the correct rate of pay.

A 1 and 2

B 1 and 3

C 2 and 3

D 3 and 4

110 Which TWO of the following controls in a purchase cycle could be implemented to reduce the risk of payment of goods not received?

1   Sequentially pre-numbered purchase requisitions and sequence check.

2   Matching of goods received note with purchase invoice.

3   Goods are inspected for condition and quantity and agreed to purchase order before acceptance.

4   Daily update of inventory system.

A   1 and 2

B   2 and 3

C   2 and 4

D   3 and 4

111 Which TWO of the following controls in the purchase cycle could be implemented to reduce the risk of procurement of unnecessary goods and services?

1   Centralised purchasing department.

2   Sequentially pre-numbered purchase requisitions and sequence check.

3   Orders can only be placed with suppliers from the approved suppliers list.

4   All purchase requisitions are signed as authorised by an appropriate manager.

A   1 and 3

B   1 and 4

C   2 and 4

D   3 and 4

112 X is a manufacturing company. It makes one product, the Y. The quality inspectors of X currently reject 3% of the finished Ys produced, as they are unfit for purpose.

Which of the following controls should reduce the rejection rate?

Select ALL that apply.

A   Increased training of quality inspectors

B   Increased training of production staff

C   Purchasing higher quality raw materials

D   Better finished goods inventory handling procedures

E   Employing more quality inspectors

113 X is a traditional retailer, specialising in sales from its physical stores. It sells a variety of products and aims to use as much of the retail space as possible to display the inventory. Impulse purchases are a common source of sales for the retailer. Unfortunately, it currently suffers significant losses due to theft by staff and customers.

Which of the following controls should reduce the number of thefts?

Select ALL that apply.

A   Employing more security guards

B   Improving staff selection procedures

C   Reducing inventory levels

D   Installing CCTV systems in stores

E   Making suppliers responsible for the cost of thefts

114 In Country A, a person over the age of 17 can drive a car on public roads only if they have passed a one hour long practical driving test with an official examiner. This test involves the candidate demonstrating several driving skills but the route and the skills chosen are at the examiner's discretion. There are 350 test centres across Country A with each employing at least 3 examiners. Examiners do not work in more than one centre.

It has been reported in the media that in some centres, fewer than 30% of candidates are passing the practical exam, whereas the pass rate is as high as 80% in others. As a result, there has been much criticism of the lack of standardisation in tests and centres with low pass rates are seeing a reduction in demand whist those with higher rates have long waiting lists.

Country A's government officials have issued a statement in response to these reports saying that, although they have the utmost faith in driving test standards in the whole of Country A, they will be implementing further standardisation measures across all centres.

Which of the following ideas for standardisation may help to reassure learner drivers the test is the same wherever it is taken?

Select ALL that apply.

A   Increase in standard examiner training periods.

B   Rotation of examiners around centres.

C   Longer tests of 90 minutes duration.

D   Increase of driving age to 18.

E   Creation of a more detailed standard list of skills needing to be demonstrated to pass the test in every location.

F   Introduction of a pass rate of 50% in each centre.

115 G is a large manufacturer of machinery which purchases oil in large quantities to use in its production processes. The oil is stored in two large tankers, referred to as A and B.

G's inventory manager has been instructed not to tie up too much cash in oil since G is currently experiencing some liquidity problems. Consequently, the inventory manager places orders for the minimum required on an ad hoc basis. G has had to postpone two large machinery orders whilst it waited for an oil delivery. The delay in delivering the orders to G's customers will result in cash penalties for G. Oil suppliers are scarce in G's home country.

The directors are concerned that, in trying to improve the liquidity position of G, they have in fact caused the situation to worsen. They have asked the inventory manager to come up with some practical ideas to prevent reoccurrence of the late delivery but also minimise liquidity risk.

Which of the following actions would be suitable suggestions for the inventory manager to make to the board?

Select ALL that apply.

A   Invest in a third tanker in order to increase stock holding capacity.

B   Establish a minimum oil inventory level at which an order will be triggered, taking into account current order requirements.

C   Negotiate shorter lead times with the oil supplier.

D   Delay payment to suppliers.

E   Find a new supplier of oil.

116   H manages a block of luxury flats at a popular coastal resort. The flats are owned by individuals who pay H to market them as holiday rentals as well as maintain them and deal with holiday makers staying in them.

H charges a flat fee for this service and also takes 10% of the holiday rental income from each booking. H insists that the owners of the flats make them available for at least 40 weeks of the year.

Any bills which are incurred for maintenance are charged back to the owners with commission of 15% and H provides a cleaning service between rentals which it also charges owners for.

H recently recruited a new office manager who decided to rearrange the filing system in the office. The manager found several invoices for maintenance work carried out by tradesmen which hadn't been recharged to clients because no specific flat address was recorded on the work done section. The office manager also found a file of invoices labelled 'miscellaneous', all paid but without sufficient detail to recharge to any flat. These invoices were mainly for small value items such as toiletries.

H's new office manager wishes to implement a new control system to ensure all costs incurred in maintaining the flats are recharged with commission to owners.

Which of the following controls would reduce the risk of costs not being correctly recharged to flat owners?

Select ALL that apply.

A   Tradesmen to be paid only on receipt of a completed standardised form showing details of flat number and work done.

B   Internally generated and sequentially numbered 'goods or service received' notes to be matched to each invoice before payment.

C   Flat owners to be charged a set amount each year to cover 'miscellaneous' items.

D   Checks carried out at the end of each month to ensure that all invoices received have been charged to a specific flat.

E   Any uncharged amounts at the end of each month to be split and recharged equally to all flats.

117 Q is a local council department which commissions services from outside contractors to carry out all aspects of the councils work. Q has a list of recommended contractors, many of whom have worked for the council for many years and provide an excellent service at a reasonable price.

Recently, central government announced changes to the health and safety laws in Q's home country. These changes meant that in order to use outside contractors, Q would need to pay for expensive insurance, or insist that contractors apply for a new Health and Safety accreditation certificate. Q does not have a budget to pay for the insurance and to qualify for the certificate contractors must pay for and attend a week long course. As yet, these courses are not available anywhere local to Q.

Central government insists that the new laws will prevent unscrupulous contractors carrying out work without proper safety controls in place. This has been a problem in some areas of the country and led to expensive compensation claims.

Which of the following are risks to Q arising from the changes to health and safety laws?

Select ALL that apply.

A   Q's contractor costs may increase.

B   Q may no longer be able to use recommended contractors.

C   There may be a shortage of contractors for Q to use leading to a backlog of work building up.

D   Q may be unable to obtain the relevant insurance.

E   Incidences of expensive compensation claims may continue to rise.

118 The following are all types of control within an organisation:

(i)   Logical access controls

(ii)   Database controls

(iii)   Hierarchical passwords

(iv)   Range checks

Which of the above controls help to ensure the security of highly confidential information?

A   (i) and (ii) only

B   (i) and (iii) only

C   (i), (ii) and (iii) only

D   All of the above

119 Foney Ltd has recently experienced a downturn in sales of their own-brand Vodka. The Marketing Director has approached the board of directors with an idea to reinvigorate the sales demand. The suggestion is that the company invests in new packaging and re-brand the Vodka to look exactly like a leading well-known brand of vodka, even using their name but selling the product to small off licenses for half the price charged by the market leader.

Which ONE following courses of actions would you suggest to the Board of Foney Ltd?

A   Implement the Marketing Director's idea as it makes strategic sense.

B   Do not proceed as it is too costly.

C   Do not proceed as the situation described by the Marketing Director is counterfeiting.

D   Do not proceed as the situation described by the Marketing Director is embezzlement.

120 Jack, a CIMA® member, has recently taken a fantastic position as finance manager for a medium-sized fashion retail company, Acia clothing plc. Jack really enjoys the job and even though the remuneration is not great, the other managers at the company have explained the way they 'get around' that issue. The sales manager explains to Jack that the key is to 'put everything on expenses – private petrol, drinks and even clothing, It's all fine and as long as you have a receipt, no-one in the finance department will question it'. The sales manager continues that 'It's fine because the board are aware of it and turn a blind eye'.

Which ONE of the following essential internal control measures is evidently missing from this company?

A   Acia lacks a control environment, Acia are without a board setting an ethical tone at the top

B   Acia lacks an Internal Audit department

C   Acia lacks an experienced finance manager

D   Acia lacks an external auditor

121 Silvermans plc, a large investment bank, has just been involved in a highly publicised fraud investigation concerning the secretary of the Board of Directors.

The investigation found that the secretary had managed to steal £2 million from the directors after they had entrusted the secretary with the ability to settle all their personal and professional financial affairs. Within a year the secretary was forging the directors' signatures and transferring monies into a private account

Which ONE of the three prerequisites for fraud have the management allowed to flourish within this situation?

A   Rationalisation

B   Motive

C   Greed

D   Opportunity

122 **Fraud risk, such as false accounting or theft of cash or assets, is one component of which type of risk?**

A   Strategic risk

B   Operational risk

C   Financial risk

D   Environmental risk

123 The Finance Director of X plc, Inaya, recently attended a CPD seminar entitled 'Fraud – How to design an anti-fraud strategy'. Inaya's original understanding of her fiduciary duty regarding fraud was that it was her job to detect any wrong doing. However the seminar enabled her to understand there are other aspects to an anti-fraud strategy.

Which of the following components are key to an effective anti-fraud strategy?

Select ALL that apply.

A   Prevention

B   Deterrence

C   Response

D   Control

124 Aggrico Bank plc has just employed a new Chief Executive Officer (CEO) after the departing Chief was convicted of a high level fraud. The new CEO has said that developing a sound ethical culture to ensure the long-term survival of the bank is vital.

Which of the following policies would help the new CEO to achieve this aim?

Select ALL that apply.

A   Establish clear anti-fraud policy statements, with explanations about acceptable behaviour.

B   A process of reminders to employees regarding fraud policy.

C   A large redundancy process to removes long-standing employees from the bank.

D   Establish a route through which suspected fraud can be reported.

125 **The primary responsibility for the prevention and detection of fraud rests with which ONE stakeholder group?**

A   The Board of Directors

B   The internal auditors

C   The external auditors

D   The Non-Executive Directors

126 Rural Ltd is an independent, small, family-owned construction business that has seen a period of rapid expansion and growth over the last five years. Until now the family have simply relied on informal trust based control systems. However, the finance officer has started to see small inventory discrepancies, the bank reconciliation not quite reconciling and the finance officer also suspects internal leaks of client information to a leading competitor.

Which of the following internal control policies would be appropriate for Rural Ltd. to implement?

Select ALL that apply.

A   Fit CCTV cameras in stockrooms

B   Requiring the division of responsibility within the purchasing process – one employee to order goods but another to authorise payment

C   Restricting personal USB drives from being brought into the office environment

D   Calling the National Crime Agency (NCA)

127 X is a hospital. In the past six months, three of the hospital staff have been attacked when walking home from work late at night.

Which of the following controls should reduce the number of attacks?

Select ALL that apply.

A   Giving all members of staff mobile telephones to report attacks

B   Providing a free bus service for staff finishing work late at night

C   Taking out insurance against attacks on staff

D   Changing the shift pattern, so staff end their shift during daylight

E   Installing floodlighting in the hospital grounds and car parks

128 EHS Co has identified that a fraud has been taking place within the organisation, and believe it has been happening for around a year. They are reviewing the staff behaviour to help assess who may have been responsible. There are four members of staff who could have perpetrated the fraud.

YS, who has worked for the company for many years, and has frequently been on performance review. The HR department of EHS have had numerous meetings and discussions with YS about not adhering to the company dress code.

JX, who is very hard working and highly thought of within EHS, often being the first one in the office in the morning, and the last one to leave. JX hasn't had a long holiday for a long time and often continues to work even when feeling poorly.

ZK, a recent hire to the organisation, who is still within the six month probationary period of their contract with EHS. This means that their work is often carried out with someone else, or reviewed by someone else once it is completed.

IO, who has never got on well with the manager of the department, and frequently complains about the support given to employees at EHS. IO is frequently off sick, citing stress as a primary factor.

Considering the fraud alerts, which ONE employee is most likely to have committed the fraud?

A   IO

B   ZK

C   JX

D   YS

129 BNG Ltd has recently discovered that it has been the victim of a false-billing fraud.

Which ONE of the following controls could BNG put in place to prevent this from occurring in the future?

A   Segregation of duties within the accounts department

B   Regular receivables ledger reconciliations

C   Authorisation of payments by management

D   Maintenance of a regular trial balance

130 Fredrickson and Co is a consultancy company that has recently seen the CEO forced to tender their resignation over serious fraud allegations. The rest of the board are looking to regain shareholder confidence.

Which THREE main fraud prevention strategies should be recommended to the Board?

A   Create and publish a whistle blowing policy

B   Do nothing, as most shareholders will probably be uninterested

C   Create a sound system of internal control

D   Create a culture that is anti-fraud with an anti-fraud 'tone at the top'

E   Announce a special dividend to be paid to all shareholders

F   Dismiss any employee who directly reported to the CEO just in case they might have been involved in any wrong doing

131 S is a multinational oil company which manages hundreds of drilling facilities across the world. S has recently undertaken a risk review of one of its major oil pipelines and as a result is keen to implement some internal control changes in order to reduce costs.

The pipeline in question runs through a remote and inhospitable country which is largely covered in ice. The pipeline is currently checked for corrosion, along its' entire length, once a week. Any signs of corrosion are treated immediately by the maintenance team carrying out the checks. If corrosion were to go untreated, the pipeline may leak resulting in catastrophic damage to the environment.

S's risk assessment suggests that instead of checking the entire pipe for corrosion each week, shorter segments should be checked instead. If the segment checked is clear of corrosion, the chances are the rest of the pipe is also clear. Over the course of a month, the entire pipe would be checked via the segment method.

The directors are very pleased with the cost savings the new internal control system will generate. The chief engineer who manages the maintenance teams is however very concerned at what could be perceived to be a dangerous reduction in controls. In the chief engineer's opinion, the risk of corrosion to the pipe is increasing as the pipe gets older and therefore extra checks should be commissioned, rather than checks reduced.

The chief engineer has asked to speak to the board about these concerns.

Which of the following statements are relevant and so should be part of the discussion?

Select ALL that apply.

A   Potential catastrophic damage to the environment caused by poor controls would increase reputation risk for S.

B   Reduced controls give the impression to maintenance staff that the risks are reduced.

C   Reporting to management on corrosion will no longer be able to take place weekly.

D   Controls should be carried out as cheaply as possible.

E   Corrosion checks should not have been considered as part of a risk assessment.

132 At a recent board meeting, the directors of R Co were discussing internal controls. The finance director was of the opinion that as long as controls were working over the recording of transactions, there was no need to implement them elsewhere in the business.

The operations director agreed, saying that controls were a financial concern and the factory floor with all of its machinery worked well because of the recruitment of experienced staff who excelled at their jobs rather than the implementation of controls.

It was true that R Co rarely had problems with machine breakdown, however theft of finished goods inventory had been an issue in the past, as had IT security. There had also been three incidences of apparently experienced staff fabricating employment history in order to get a job at R Co. The CEO argued that these problems could be prevented from happening again with the introduction of new controls but the operational director disagreed saying these examples just represented risks of being in business.

Which of the following controls, if implemented, could help prevent one or more of the incidences described from reoccurring?

Select ALL that apply.

A Quality and quantity checks on receipt of raw materials before goods receipt notes signed.

B Key pad protected access to all inventory storage areas with frequent code changes.

C References from two most recent jobs requested and checked for all new recruits.

D Individual password protected access to all computer systems with passwords changed frequently.

E Quality checks on finished goods before delivery to customers

133 B Company operates car parks across most of the major cities and airports of Country C. At a recent senior management meeting, one of the area managers with responsibility for 20 car parks stated that they had some concerns about revenue collection in the car parks and also security.

The area manager explained that in some of the car parks, the automatic ticket machines which recorded entrance times of vehicles ran out of paper frequently and cars were unable to enter the car park until they were refilled. This often caused traffic jams on entry at busy times.

In addition, the automatic payment machines at the exits always took payment but often ran out of paper to issue receipts to customers when car parks were busy. Although there were signs on the car park entrances stating that cars were left at customers own risk, the occasional vandalism within car parks was occurring and despite the CCTV installed, customers could be put off using them after hours.

Due to recent redundancies and staff sickness, it was difficult to ensure a member of staff was always on site to deal with these issues when they occurred. Often single car park attendants were left with responsibility for the days takings when waiting for the security firm to collect the cash.

Which of the following control weaknesses are likely to lead directly to lost revenue within the car parks?

Select ALL that apply.

A   Delay in refilling paper in automatic ticket machines.

B   Delay in refilling paper in automatic payment machines.

C   Single member of staff responsible for takings until security firm arrives.

D   Occasional vandalism to cars.

E   Staff sickness and redundancies.

F   Lack of attendant on site at all times.

134   Many organisations consider outsourcing their Internal Audit function.

Which of the following are ADVANTAGES of doing this?

Select ALL that apply.

A   Specialist skills may be more readily available

B   Risk of staff turnover is passed to the outsourcing firm

C   Better understanding of the organisation's objectives and culture

D   May improve independence

E   Decisions relating to Internal Audit can be based solely on cost

135   Many organisations consider outsourcing their Internal Audit function.

Which of the following are DISADVANTAGES of doing this?

Select ALL that apply.

A   Flexibility and availability may not be as high as with an in-house function

B   Decisions relating to Internal Audit may be based solely on cost

C   Increased management time

D   Possible conflict of interest if provided by the external auditors

E   Loss of control over standard of service

136   Internal and external audit have similarities, but several features distinguish between them.

Drag and drop the following distinguishing features into the correct category.

	Internal Audit	External Audit
Required by shareholders		
Required by statute		
Reports to Shareholders and Management		
Reports to Audit Committee or Directors		
Reports on financial statements		
Reports on controls		

137 Jan has been invited to run her company's first Internal Audit department. Jan is currently discussing plans for the department with the Finance Director, who is Jan's existing line manager. The Finance Director has made a number of suggestions but Jan is worried they might contravene Internal Audit Attribute Standards.

For each suggestion identify which Internal Audit Attribute Standards are being contravened, if any:

Suggestion
It should not be a problem that Jan has no experience of audit and is only part-qualified.
The first project for the new department should be to audit the Treasury Department, which Jan currently manages.
Jan, as Head of Internal Audit, should report to the Finance Director.

Internal Audit Attribute Standard contravened
Independence
Objectivity
Professional Care
None contravened

138 Portland plc has a well-established internal audit department consisting of staff that have an average length of service of six years. The scope of the internal auditors work is determined by the Chief Financial Officer (CFO). For some projects the internal audit teams review their own work.

Which of the following statements are correct?

1 The independence of the internal audit department could be enhanced if another member of the finance team was involved in determining the scope of their work.

2 To eliminate any self-review threats Portland plc could increase expenditure on training so that internal auditors are better able to identify errors in their own work.

3 Staff should be rotated on a regular basis to reduce the familiarity threat associated with the long length of service.

A Both 1 and 2

B 2 only

C Both 1 and 3

D 3 only

139 FTS plc is planning to introduce a new benchmarking procedure as part of internal audit to help identify risk areas but is unsure which type of benchmarking would be most appropriate. It is aware that each type of benchmarking has certain drawbacks.

FTS has identified that _____1_____ benchmarking is often difficult to undertake as it is difficult to convince the other party to share information about their operations.

_____2_____ benchmarking is unlikely to suggest any strategic risks for the whole organisation and is typically only useful where the organisation feels that conformity of service is crucial to its operations.

Finally, _____3_____ benchmarking often fails to provide data on the benchmarking company's core functions as it requires the organisation to benchmark itself against an organisation in a different industry.

Use the options below to fill in the missing words in gaps 1, 2 and 3.

A   Process

B   Internal

C   Competitive

140   Which of the following is an example of an analytical review procedure?

A   Comparing gross profit margin to the prior year figure to identify significant changes

B   Enquiries of management regarding the risks of the business

C   Observation of internal control procedures

D   Recalculation of a balance

141   Moyles Co operate a chain of car dealerships and has a large internal audit department in place. The management of Moyles Co are keen to increase the range of assignments that internal audit undertake.

Which TWO of the following assignments could the internal audit department of Moyles Co be asked to perform by management?

1   Fill a temporary vacancy in the credit control department on a rotational basis.

2   Under the external auditor's supervision, assist the external auditors by evaluating returns from the receivables circularisation.

3   Implement a new inventory control system.

4   Evaluate the inventory count instructions.

A   1 and 2

B   3 and 4

C   2 and 4

D   1 and 3

142   Carson plc is a small family-run company selling fishing tackle and bait from a small chain of shops. The firm has seen rapid sales growth since engaging in e-commerce via a website and selling via large online auction sites.

The newly appointed Finance Director is the only Board member from outside the family and has suggested it would be a good idea for Carson plc to consider establishing an internal audit department as a large inventory discrepancy for fishing clothing has recently been discovered.

Which THREE of the following factors are the main reasons for the need for an internal audit at Carson plc?

A   The fact the board has majority family members

B   If a company is listed on the stock exchange it must have an internal audit

C   The growing scale and variety of selling channels suggests there is a higher risk of error

D   Potential internal control issues are starting to arise

E   The introduction of e-commerce

F   The wish of shareholders

143 B Retail has discovered that staff have been excessively discounting stock for sale to friends and family at 2 stores. This is against B retail's staff policies and procedures. They would like their internal audit department to look into this issue at their other 25 stores.

Which of the following types of audit would be applicable?

Select ALL that apply.

A   Compliance audit

B   Management audit

C   Systems audit

D   Risk based audit

E   Environmental audit

144 Which of the systems below would be audited as a "systems-based audit"?

A   Sales ledger system

B   EPOS (Electronic point of sale) system

C   Non-current asset recording

D   All of the above

145 Once an audit is completed an audit report is issued. Which of the following are appropriate features of an audit report?

Select ALL that apply.

A   Recommendations for action

B   Audit opinion/grading of the area/system reviewed

C   Results of tests carried out

D   Objectives of the audit

E   Summary of the audit process for this audit

146 The directors of BGT have decided to create an internal audit department and in line with company policy, they are keen to promote staff from within BGT to work in the new department.

The finance director has some reservations about this as a team made up of internal staff will lack independence. The other directors believe that this drawback will be outweighed by the new department's knowledge of BGT which will enable them to become effective much more quickly. There are however some reservations about the availability of internal candidates.

Which of the following factors are arguments the finance director can use to persuade the board that BGT should recruit external candidates into the new internal audit function?

Select ALL that apply.

A   External recruits will view BGT with a 'fresh pair of eyes' and so be able to more effectively recognise risk.

B   External recruits will not be at risk of reviewing their own work.

C   Internal recruits may find it harder to adopt an attitude of professional scepticism towards their colleagues.

D   External recruits will have a better balance of skills than internal candidates.

E   Internal promotion will be quicker.

147   X outsources its internal audit work to a local firm of accountants Z. The manager in Z who is responsible for co-ordinating the work done at X has arranged an annual review meeting with the directors of X to discuss the controls work carried out by Z over the last year and any further projects for Z going forward.

At the meeting, the board of directors explained that two instances of fraud had been discovered by their external auditors during the yearend audit. On both occasions the fraud concerned staff ordering computers for their own use through the company's procurement system. It would seem they were able to do this because the system allowed access without a password and could be operated from any computer in the accounts office.

The directors wished to know why Z had not remedied this control weakness during the review of internal controls commissioned last year.

The manager from Z pointed out that a lack of controls over purchasing had been flagged in their report but that as internal auditors they were not responsible for remedying problems.

The directors are questioning whether to dispense with the services of Z on the basis of this statement.

Which of the following actions could Z have carried out over the last year to reduce the risk of fraud occurring?

Select ALL that apply.

A   Z could have acted as a deterrent to staff perpetrating fraud.

B   Z could have suggested improvements to the purchasing system.

C   Z could have implemented controls to prevent access to the purchasing system without a password.

D   Z could have detected and investigated fraud.

E   Z could have provided information to be used in the external audit.

148 GAT is a listed company which manufactures complex engineering products. The organisation has been performing very strongly in some new overseas markets over the last year and consequently sales have increased considerably.

A new system for recording sales is currently being installed to cater for the increased number of transactions within the company. Staff training on the new system has yet to be carried out and the Finance Director has some concerns that the changeover from the old system will result in information being lost.

Until a year ago, GAT employed a qualified accountant as an internal auditor however when this person left a replacement was not hired. The Board are now considering a request from the finance director to set up an internal audit department to help with the new systems and ensure controls over sales are adequate. The board are reluctant to authorise the expense of recruiting internal audit staff.

Which of the following factors are arguments the finance director can use to persuade the board that GAT should have an internal audit function?

Select ALL that apply.

A   Internal audit can manage the sales function and ensure sales are not understated.

B   Shareholders will be reassured by the presence of internal audit.

C   Internal audit can help with the systems changeover and work to ensure controls over sales are robust.

D   Not replacing the internal auditor a year ago contravened listing rules.

E   GAT has grown in size and become more complex. This suggests it will require more monitoring going forward to reduce risks of fraud and error.

149 BBD Ltd is a web design company and after several years of sustained growth it has decided to continue its growth it is time to set up an internal audit department.

It has successfully recruited an internal audit team and they are due to start working on their first assignment. The manager of the department to be audited is quite anxious about the prospect as it will be a new experience, the manager is concerned the audit report will criticise the department they are responsible for, it will damage their own reputation and they won't have any opportunity to respond.

Which of the following statements are true regarding best practice for the audit report and will help reduce the managers concerns?

Select ALL that apply.

A   The points raised in the audit report should be discussed with manager of the department being audited before they are reported.

B   The manager will be able to ask for any points they dislike to be removed from the audit report before it is submitted.

C   The internal audit report will be remain confidential within the organisation after it has been submitted.

D   The audit report will include recommendations for action and they should be practical and cost-effective.

E   The manager of the department being audited can comment on the points in the report and the comments will be added to the report.

CYBER RISKS

150 As more and more business activity is carried out online, organisations hold more and more information on their systems that would be appealing to criminals.

Which THREE of the following are the main types of sensitive information?

A   Personal information

B   Classified information

C   Secret recipes

D   Employee information

E   Business information

151 Social engineering relates to the theory of influence, according to Dr Robert Cialdini there are six principles used to persuade or influence someone.

Which of the following are included in the six principles?

Select ALL that apply.

A   Consensus

B   Scarcity

C   Authenticity

D   Consistency

E   Integrity

F   Reciprocity

152 The Senior Finance Manager at Hackers Ltd received an email that appeared to be from BST, Hackers' bank. The email asked for the manager to confirm some of the security in formation, by clicking on a link and answering some questions. At the end of the week, one of the manager's direct reports flagged some unusual transactions while carrying out routine bank reconciliations. There were several large payments to unknown sources.

Which ONE of the following cyber-attacks does it appear that Hackers Ltd were a victim of?

A   Keylogging

B   Botnets

C   Sceenshotting

D   Phishing

E   Distributed denial of service

153 GHU Company wishes to protect itself against cyber-attacks and has been reviewing the cyber risks it faces. One risk is has identified is that the financial data it holds electronically and uses for financial reporting purposes could be improperly modified.

Which ONE of the following cyber security objectives would be threatened if this risk was realised?

A   Availability

B   Confidentiality

C   Integrity of data

D   Integrity of processing

154 HHP Company makes customised flower arrangements. The flowers are ordered by customers to mark or celebrate significant events and are despatched to nominated recipients with a message card completed by the customer.

Which TWO of the following pieces of sensitive information held by HHP constitute Personal Information?

A   Delivery addresses

B   Product specifications

C   Quarterly sales forecasts

D   Average customer feedback scores

E   Message card contents

155 BBJ Company employs an external call centre to process its customer service call handling.

When evaluating the characteristics of BBJ that could give rise to cybersecurity threats, the call centre is an example of which type of characteristic?

A   Type of technology used

B   Type of connection to technology

C   Service providers used

D   Delivery channels used

156 The board of GJH Company have approved a number of proposals to be completed in the next period.

Which THREE of the following proposals would have an impact on the company's cyber-security risk?

A   Changing the specification of their best-selling product

B   Acquiring a new manufacturing facility

C   Revaluing non-current assets

D   Outsourcing the Human Resources department

E   Replacing laptops used by the sales force

157 FFK Company is a small manufacturing company supplying wholesale customers who order goods by phone. It operates from one site and has its own internal accounts department. Labels for goods to be despatched are printed on-site and the goods are then collected by a local courier service for delivery. Inventory levels for key components are monitored electronically and suppliers receive automatic notification when deliveries are required.

Based on the information provided, which ONE of the following features of FFK Company's business model are MOST likely to expose them to cyber-security threats?

A   Orders placed by phone

B   Internal accounts department

C   Use of a local courier service

D   Inventory arrangement with component suppliers

158 BKL Company is a small manufacturer of frozen organic meals. It has previously used a wholesaler to distribute its products but has now decided to market direct to customers. The IT director has therefore persuaded the board that a 'BKL meals' page containing information about the company's products should be set up on a well-known social networking site.

Which of the following opportunities and risks would arise if the social media page was set up by BKL?

Select ALL that apply.

A   Increasing brand awareness

B   Chance to screen potential job candidates

C   Increased vulnerability to denial of service (DoS) attacks

D   Reputational damage due to inactivity

E   Greater access to customer feedback

159 PHK Company sells high-end jewellery to retail customers via its website. It then uses DDD, an external courier, to deliver the orders to its customers. Hackers, who wished to steal their customers' addresses, inserted malicious code into an unprotected password input box on PHK's website and successfully accessed and copied the addresses from PHK's database.

This attack on PKH by the hackers is an example of which of the following cyber-risks?

Select ALL that apply.

A   Theft of personal information

B   Exploitation of external delivery channels

C   Malvertising

D   Structured Query Language (SQL) injection attack

E   Spear phishing

160 When a new information system is being developed, or an existing system revised, such development should be carefully controlled.

Which of the following are examples of system development controls?

Select ALL that apply.

A System testing

B Training

C Formal authorisation of system design

D System documentation

E Passwords

161 ACI Ltd sells fresh fruit and vegetable boxes to customers in the local area. ACI has had incredible success and based on customer feedback has decided to set up a website to allow customers to order online. The main concern with this is that, because ACI operates in a remote location, the internet access it has can be intermittent and slow, leading to the website crashing if too many requests come through at the same time.

Which ONE of the following cyber security objectives would be threatened if this was realised?

A Availability

B Confidentiality

C Integrity of data

D Integrity of processing

162 X is a multi-site organisation, formed by the recent merger of five organisations. Each site currently uses a different information system for the recording and processing of raw material inventory. It is planned to replace these systems with one new system that will be common to every site.

Which of the following system changeover methods may be used?

Select ALL that apply.

A Direct

B Parallel

C Pilot

D Phased

163 Flossy Mossy Ltd (FM) have decided to try and capitalise on the growing trend for online orders and home delivery by offering a courier service on top of their other services. It has hired a consultant to help review risks.

Which of the following statements made by the consultant are describing cyber risk?

Select ALL that apply.

A   If a courier does not take appropriate care they could be watched working on their tablet while they are on their rounds, giving away sensitive data about customers and FM operations

B   One of FM's competitors could attempt to disrupt communications with consumers and couriers to delay services and damage reputation

C   A competitor could advertise on a major website to try and gain market share

D   A courier could mislay their tablet, and jeopardise sensitive data that FM holds about customers

E   An individual could deliberately create an overwhelming wave of internet traffic on one of FM's sites using botnets

164 When an organisation undertakes changes as it carries out its business activities it can make changes that could impact its cyber security risks.

Which of the following are changes that would necessarily affect cyber security risk management?

Select ALL that apply.

A   A business acquires a competitor

B   A large training organisation changes it's organisational structure from divisional based on geography to a matrix structure.

C   A local market trader decides who usually works Monday to Friday decides to open a operate at a new Sunday market.

D   A window cleaning business changes from accepting cash only to allowing customer to pay online.

E   The board of a large retailer decide that the culture of the organisation is no longer appropriate and have decided to lead by example in changing the organisational culture.

165 Direct changeover is assumed to be the highest risk alternative available.

Which TWO of the following controls can mitigate the risk of system failure when a direct changeover is used?

A   Testing

B   Training

C   System documentation

D   Data backup

E   Check digits

166   **EU Member States can introduce exemptions from the GDPR's transparency obligations. Which of the following are acceptable reasons that member states can have exemptions?**

Select ALL that apply.

A   Bank records

B   National security

C   National defence

D   Public security

E   Election campaigns

167   One of the common forms of cyber attack is application attack.

Which of the following are forms of applications attacks?

Select ALL that apply.

A   Ransomware

B   Trojans

C   SQL injection

D   Buffer overflow

E   Ethical hacking

168   Four Folks Inc (FF) is restaurant chain based in the developed and prosperous country of Usland. FF specialise producing high quality burgers that are both meat and dairy free.

FF was established by four friends who went to university together and were all vegan. Frustrated that the fast food industry was dominated by meat options and disappointed by the meat and dairy free alternatives available in the traditional fast food outlets, they decided to open a restaurant in the city of Few Pork when they left university over 15 years ago. The restaurant sells high-quality vegan burgers that are cooked to order and can be eaten in comfortable, good quality surroundings, or taken away.

At first FF had modest success, but as awareness of veganism grew, it has expanded rapidly over the last 5 years. It now operates across Usland and have recently opened its first restaurants overseas, expanding into another well developed country, Ukland based in the EU. FF has always been very active on social media, raising awareness of the brand through this, but also monitoring customer feedback.

As well as overseas expansion, FF has also embraced technological advancements and launched an application (app) that can be used by customers on smartphones, tablets and computers. To use the app, customers must set up an account by providing basic details (name, age, gender, employment status, address, and email address).

Customers can use the app for a variety of purposes, to place an order for a take-away, to book a table for a meal (subject to availability), to pre-order the meal and to provide feedback on the meal. The booking of a table and ordering of a meal must be done at least 15 minutes prior to the arrival time. This means that the table and meal can both be ready for the customer as soon as they arrive, leading to better resource management for FF and reduced waiting times for the customer.

Which of the following statements are true?

Select ALL that apply.

A   The expansion overseas is an change that could increase the cyber security risks of FF

B   The introduction of the app would impact the cyber risks that FF faces

C   All of the basic details that the customer must provide to FF to the app represent PII

D   As the app incorporates feedback, FF do not need to monitor social media anymore

E   As an account is created by the customer, FF do not need to worry about the integrity of data

F   As FF are based in Usland they do not need to worry about GDPR legislation

169   SiberSink Co offer smart plumbing accessories that can be controlled from a smartphone application. One of its bestselling products is a bath accessories set that allows the user to start running the bath remotely, apparently it is most commonly started from the users bed. SiberSink has recently suffered an SQL injection attack.

Which ONE of the following best describes the attack?

A   Personal and business information held on the system has been stolen.

B   The company computer system has been shut down until a payment has been made.

C   An attacker found an unprotected input box on the company website, executed a query and gained access to their database of customer details.

D   Attackers identified the identity of the finance director, found out their personal interests through social media and then sent them an email specific to their interests with a malicious link in it.

170   PII is a valuable commodity for cyber criminals.

Which ONE of the following is the place where PII is most likely to be traded?

A   The deep web

B   The tor web

C   The surface web

D   The sinister web

E   The dark web

171   **Which ONE of the following is the best definition of polymorphic malware?**

A   A type of malware that avoids being identified by systems and networks by constantly changing its identifiable features

B   A type of malware that records every keystroke typed by the victim

C   An issue within some software that is known to the developer but has been left unaddressed

D   A type of malware that specifically targets the banking industry due to a banks perceived attractiveness for attack from criminals

172 A way to carry out phishing. Sometimes referred to as CEO fraud because it can involve someone impersonating a CEO and asking for a particular action or piece of information to be sent through.

Which ONE of the following is this a description of?

A   Domain fraud

B   Business Email Compromise

C   Buffer overflow attack

D   Malvertising

173 **Which of the following are reasons for social engineering being so important in cyber security?**

Select ALL that apply.

A   It's not really relevant

B   Employees often do not feel they are part of the security systems

C   People are seen as more susceptible to attacks than computer systems and programmes

D   Ethical hackers like to collect PII and sell it on the dark web

E   Weaponised documents don't work anymore

174 CXD Company has a network configuration management (NCM) system in place.

Which ONE of the following benefits would be associated with NCM system?

A   Automatic back-up of all files containing important information

B   Identification of any components of the IT system which have not run software updates

C   Prevention of data modification without the consent of all participants in the network

D   Analysis of patterns in the data held by the system

175 **Which of the following would be recommended to a business to help reduce cyber risks?**

Select ALL that apply.

A   Regular IT training for staff

B   Implementing access controls

C   Ensure all staff to use the same memorable password so that people don't forget it

D   Use patch management to keep software security up to date

E   Establish and communicate IT policies and procedures

F   Allowing all staff the freedom to use social media without any limitations to help motivate them

176 HJK is a small company which supplies components to the motor industry. Because the market in which it operates is highly competitive, the board believes any systems failures could lead to lost contracts and the company must therefore have a robust IT disaster recovery plan.

Which ONE of the following actions would be MOST likely to be included in a disaster recovery plan?

A   Using a cloud-based data back-up service

B   Ensuring all anti-virus software is up to date

C   Introducing centralised monitoring of systems activity

D   Protecting secure information with an SSL certificate

177 VHJ Company is keen to protect the company system from cyber-attack and has therefore introduced unique access codes for all employees to use when logging on to the system.

What form of cyber-protection do unique access codes represent?

A   Identification

B   Authentication

C   Authorisation

D   Certification

178 JR has just started working for EWI Plc. As part of EWI's on boarding process it requires all new starters to attend a morning session about the purpose, values and principles of the organisation. EWI take cyber risk very seriously and the afternoon is dedicated to cyber security on boarding. Part of the cyber security on boarding includes logging on to their new laptop and setting up their profile, included in this EWI explain password best practice to their new hires.

JR has chosen the following password: JR1998&EWI.

Which of the following statements are correct regarding JR's password?

Select ALL that apply.

A   JR should write it down to make sure they do not forget it

B   Once it is set, JR should send an email to IT confirming the password so they have it for their records.

C   The password would be improved by including some lower case characters

D   The password appears to be significant, and could therefore be more easily guessed

E   The password is a reasonable length

179 In response to concerns about an increased risk of cyber-attacks LPK Company has set up a security operations centre (SOC).

Which ONE of the following objectives BEST describe the aims of an SOC?

A   To monitor an organisation's systems, defend it against breaches in security, and identify and mitigate security risks

B   To monitor LPK's compliance with International Organisation for Standardisation (ISO) 27001

C   To respond to cyber-security breaches and ensure business continuity in the event of a cyber-attack

D   To provide a fully functioning back-up computer and network operations site in the event of a disaster

180 **Which of the following would be likely to be included in an IT policy document advising on password security?**

Select ALL that apply.

A   Use the same passwords for work and personal accounts, to make it easier for you to remember it

B   When the IT department ask for your password to work on your PC you must always give it to them

C   Keep a list of all your passwords either in your desk or another convenient location in case you forget them

D   Create strong passwords that are difficult to guess

E   Password321 is a stronger password than S9v£E1X

181 BDG Company has asked its cyber-security team to improve its endpoint security.

Which ONE of the following features of BDG's systems is MOST likely to give rise to a need for greater endpoint security?

A   System now allows customers to purchase goods via BDG's web pages

B   System holds higher levels of confidential information

C   Significant numbers of remote devices now accessing the network

D   A far greater number of transactions are forecast in the forthcoming period

182 One of the responses that an organisation can have in place to help with cyber security risk management is back ups.

Which ONE of the following is a type of back up?

A   Reflective site

B   Arctic back up site

C   Buffer overflow back up site

D   Warm back up site

183 Engine4.com Ltd is an airline operator based in the north of Ukland, it has previously specialised in short haul flights to destinations within Ukland. After a recent review of performance, the company decided to offer long haul flights to expand their business. The board decided that a strategic alliance would be an appropriate way to start this venture and they are close to an arrangement with Longhaul Ltd.

The board are concerned that as part of this arrangement they will, for the first time, have to send confidential information about its passengers and employees to a third party.

Which of the following cyber security tools appropriate to ensure that only the intended recipient is able to access the confidential information?

Select ALL that apply.

A   Using a mirror site back up

B   Using antivirus and endpoint security products

C   Segmenting the network using network configurations management

D   Encrypting the data

E   Annual cyber security training for all Engine4.com staff

184 Montyrubble is a chocolatier based in the prosperous country of Fraland. It set up in 20X2 and has enjoyed a lot of success since then. Its focus has primarily been on making sales to individual consumers through its ever expanding number of shops, but also through online sales and delivery.

At a recent meeting, the senior management decided to start selling to other businesses either for sales in appropriate stores that fitted with their upmarket image, or as gifts for hardworking employees.

During the meeting the IT manager suggested that the company should work towards ISO27001 compliance.

Which of the following are the MOST likely reasons for the IT manager suggesting becoming ISO27001 compliant?

Select ALL that apply.

A   The IT manager needs more work

B   Some organisations require B2B partners to be ISO27001 compliant to do business with them

C   ISO27001 ensures a proactive approach to cyber security risk management

D   Chocolate retailers are known to be particularly susceptible to cyber risks

E   Being ISO27001 will mean Montyrubble no longer needs to worry about cyber risks

185 BUS Ltd is a training organisation based in Gerland, the board are becoming increasingly concerned about cyber threats. The IT manager has proposed that as part of an increased focus on network configurations management the organisation could ban the use of USB drives on work computers.

The board are reluctant to sanction this because the use of USB drives is widespread by their employees and they feel it will meet with significant resistance from employees.

Which of the following statements given by the IT manager about why USB devices should be banned are correct?

Select ALL that apply.

A   USB drives could contain malware and when inserted into a network device, the malware could infect BUS Ltd systems.

B   Sensitive information could be stolen from BUS Ltd by employees using USB drives.

C   There are no controls that could protect sensitive information from being stolen on a USB drive.

D   Antivirus software may not be able to prevent malware from a USB drive.

E   Employees losing USB drives containing sensitive information also presents a cyber risk to BUS Ltd

186 BKL Company is a large manufacturing company supplying components to vehicle manufacturers. It works closely with its customers offering services such as just-in-time deliveries and integrated inventory ordering systems. It has a large sales force which travels to current and potential clients logging on to the company network from tablets or laptops.

The company has recently recovered from a malware attack and wishes to identify how the malware entered the system.

Which ONE of the following strategies would be MOST suitable to enable BKL to achieve this objective?

A   Introduce a blockchain system between the companies in the supply chain

B   Conduct penetration testing of the network

C   Employ specialists to reverse engineer the malware identified in the system

D   Identify all the devices which are connected to the network

187 CHU Company is working to improve its cyber security risk management and wishes to start by identifying which of the staff groups within the organisation should be tasked with minimising the company's cyber security risk.

Which of the following staff groups should be instructed to work to minimise CHU's cyber security risk?

Select ALL that apply.

A   Board of Directors

B   Systems and Organisation Controls (SOC) team

C   Information Technology (IT) department

D   Operational staff

E   Senior management

188 GHJ Company is concerned that the company's systems are at risk of cyber attack. Two specific areas of concern are the on-line payment systems used by customers and the use of remote devices by the company's sales force.

Which TWO of the following types of penetration test would be most suitable to assess the vulnerability of GHJ to the cyber risks associated with their two areas of concern?

A   Infrastructure penetration test

B   Internal network penetration test

C   Web application penetration test

D   Wireless network penetration test

E   Simulated phishing test

189 The board of YRV Company is concerned that confidential information which has been deleted from its systems may still be recoverable if the company was subject to a cyber attack and intend to employ specialist forensic analysts to assist them.

Which ONE of the following forms of analysis should the board request in order to determine whether the deleted information could still be accessed via a cyber attack?

A   System level analysis

B   Storage analysis

C   Network analysis

D   Malware analysis

190 YWT Company has been victim of a malware cyber attack and a forensic analysis is in operation. The company is currently running a system level analysis.

Which THREE of the following objectives would be most likely to be included in a system level analysis?

A   Discovering the what the malware was intended to achieve

B   Recognising fake accounts created to allow the hacker access to the system

C   Detecting configuration changes arising as a result of the attack

D   Determining how the malware was infiltrated the system

E   Identifying changes to the components of the operating system

191 Vera Inc is a cyber security firm that helps with protection techniques, but their main focus is in assisting with specialised responses to cyber security breaches that have occurred. They offer penetration testing and have highly skilled employees in their firm.

Which TWO of the following statements are correct?

A   Vera Inc must have a very careful recruitment selection criteria and internal controls as its employees could have ulterior motives to be involved in penetration testing at Vera's clients.

B   The work carried out by Vera Inc for its clients will prevent their clients from being subject to cyber attacks.

C   Vera Inc itself is unlikely to be subject to cyber attack and even if it was hacked it could just cover it up to avoid anyone finding out about it.

D   As well as penetration testing, specialised responses are likely to include forensic analysis, blockchain and malware analysis.

E   The protection techniques that Vera Inc could sell include employee training, certification and antivirus endpoint security.

192 F&T Co is a small family owned business making sandwiches and cakes for sale in their local region. The company has a head office, a small factory and two shops. The four sites while in fairly close proximity are all linked by the company's computer systems to help efficient stock control. This is important as it produces is perishable and it needs to avoid wastage.

As F&T has a small seating area in each shop, the two shops offer free customer Wi-Fi.

The small board of F&T is meeting to discuss the cyber risks they face.

Which of the following statements that were made at the meeting are true?

Select ALL that apply.

A   Now our staff have been trained on email use and phishing, F&T Co will be protected from cyber attacks as long as our staff do not open emails from senders they do not recognise

B   We only need to worry about external threats to our IT systems

C   The new antivirus software that we installed should help prevent our systems from being attacked

D   Implementing network configuration management to segment our Wi-Fi network so that the customers cannot access the same areas as our staff was a sensible decision

E   Paying someone to monitor the data moving across our network is a waste of resources and time

193 The board of HYN Plc have met recently to discuss cyber risks and think that HYN Plc need to make some improvements to their cyber security processes.

Which of the following statements made by the directors of HYN Plc about cyber security are correct?

Select ALL that apply.

A   The need for security processes is decreasing and there is little to be gained from someone attacking our systems

B   Using network configuration management to segment the network would help with cyber security at HYN Plc

C   Penetration testing can include allowing someone basic internal network access and seeing if they can gain unauthorised access to sensitive information

D   The internet of things is irrelevant to HYN Plc as it is only to do with devices around the home like smart speakers

E   Business process controls are an important tool in strengthening our defences against cyber risk, it's not all about encryption and antivirus software

194 JZZ Plc is dairy business based in Swemark, it supplies dairy products to businesses across the EU, and their biggest customers are supermarkets. It works closely with supermarkets to make sure they have fresh supplies arriving regularly throughout the week to their many stores. As such JZZ Plc has integrated ordering systems to enable easy ordering for its customers and prompt delivery to the appropriate outlets across Europe.

The company has recently been subject to a SQL injection attack, where a hacker found an unprotected input box and injected malicious code into the database from the unprotected input box. The board are currently reviewing the cyber security processes in place and considering how they could improve their cyber security.

Which of the following statements would be appropriate steps to help reduce the likelihood of such attacks in future?

Select ALL that apply.

A   Web application penetration testing

B   Hiring an unethical hacker

C   IT training for all staff to reduce the likelihood of staff clicking on malicious links

D   Review the business continuity plans they have in place

E   Prohibit the use of BYOD at JZZ.

195   DMY Inc has recently suffered a cyber breach and it has hired a cyber security firm to assist with the response. It had been worried about a possible breach and so the IT department had recently moved some files containing confidential business information to a new and more secure cloud server. Despite the files having been deleted from the servers, DMY is concerned they may still have been accessible.

DMY has asked the cyber security firm to carry out a forensic analysis.

Which ONE area of the forensic analysis would be MOST likely to identify if the files were accessed?

A   Reverse engineering

B   System level analysis

C   Storage analysis

D   Network analysis

196   HLP Company is a large multi-national retail chain. It is compiling a cyber security risk management report for relevant stakeholders.

Under the AICPA 2017 cyber security risk management reporting framework, which of the following events should be disclosed in their report?

Select ALL that apply.

A   An attempted cyber attack on the company's systems that was identified and prevented before it accessed the system

B   The purchase of additional word processing software licences to support the growth of its customer service department

C   The publishing of a report by HLP's Internal Audit department into the results of its cyber security vulnerability assessment

D   The detailed work carried out by HLP's cyber security team to strengthen the system against a new virus reported by industry insiders

E   The passing of a board resolution to outsource product distribution to an external delivery service

197 PAR Company sells garden furniture via its website and takes payment details via a secure on-line payment service.

The cyber risk reporting team at PAR is writing a paragraph on the company's approach to the management of cyber risk for inclusion in the Customers' Frequently Asked Questions page on the company's website.

Which ONE of the following descriptions of PAR Company's cyber security risk management would be MOST relevant for inclusion?

A   Types of technologies used by the company systems

B   Employee policies for cyber security training

C   The company's cyber security confidentiality objective

D   The nature of the company's business operations

198 DYT Company is compiling the contents for inclusion in its 'Description of DYT Company's cybersecurity risk management programme using the AICPA 2017 cyber security risk management reporting framework.

Which ONE of the following matters should be included in the section on DYT's Risk Governance Structure?

A   Measures identified to prevent unauthorised access to confidential information

B   Identification and evaluation of the risks which can be mitigated by the purchase of insurance

C   Review meetings between the board and the Systems and Organisation Controls (SOC) team

D   Details of strategic decisions resulting in expansion of the network

199 RTW Company has entered into a new joint arrangement with an external accounting firm which will now be responsible for all aspects of the company's payroll and management accounting.

The company cyber risk security team is now considering the content to be included in its report 'Description of RTW Company's cyber security risk management program' which is to be produced in accordance with the AICPA 2017 cyber security risk management reporting framework.

Under which ONE of the following headings within the report would the specifics of this new arrangement need to be described?

A   Cyber security objectives

B   Factors affecting inherent cyber security risks

C   Cyber security risk assessment process

D   Cyber security control processes

200 The management of LPU Company is in the process of finalising their cyber security risk management report, which is being produced in accordance with the AICPA 2017 cyber security risk management reporting framework.

Under the framework, which ONE of the following practitioners should be appointed by the board to provide an opinion on the description of LPU's cyber security risk management programme and the effectiveness of its controls?

A   A qualified auditor

B   A certified public accountant (CPA)

C   A chartered IT professional (CITP)

D   LPU's chief information security officer (CISO)

201 There are now several different frameworks available relating to cyber security to assist organisations with their cyber security processes.

Which of the following are inherent limitations of frameworks?

Select ALL that apply.

A   They do not give guidance on how to prevent and prepare for cyber attacks

B   Cyber risks are ever changing and they cannot predict new forms of attack

C   They do not help organisations defend against all forms of attack.

D   They only focus on prevention of attack

E   They cannot completely eliminate the risk of cyber attack

202 DRF Ltd has been increasing its focus on cyber security as some of its competitors have suffered cyber attack. The IT manager proposed that DRF should launch a digital resilience programme and after discussions with other senior managers, the board at DRF agreed it was a good approach to take.

Work on the digital resilience programme has been under way for some time now, the board are satisfied that they have investigated and identified the risks that DRF faces, and they have agreed the programme objectives. The IT manager has created four alternative options regarding the level of prevention that DRF could undertake, and an estimated cost to implement for each option, the board have decided which option they think is most appropriate, but have yet to communicate this to the IT manager.

The IT manager has also been working with HR to consider how they could use the appraisal process to help ensure sustained motivation towards cyber security, regardless of the level of prevention the board ultimately choose.

Using the six step approach to digital resilience, which of the following steps are still to be considered?

Select ALL that apply.

A   Identify all the issues

B   Aim towards a well defined target

C   Work out how best to deliver the new cyber security system

D   Establish the risk resource trade offs

E   Develop a plan that aligns business and technology

F   Ensure sustained business engagement

203 The board of TSN Ltd have been discussing improving their responses to the increasing threat from cyber risks, one of the board suggested using the AIC Triad as a framework.

As a result of this conversation they have been working on various aspects, they have set up a mirror site for their retail website, the have both a disaster recovery plan and business continuity plan in place and have in place a daily scan for updates to make sure any software security patches are applied without delay. They have also started using end to end encryption for all messages that are sent either internally or externally and a policy in place for all new recruits to be trained on social engineering and password best practice, with regular update trainings for existing employees.

Despite the progress they have made all staff have access to perform any action on any customer record in their database, and they can all create new customers should they need to.

Which ONE aspect of the AIC Triad do TSN need to improve on the most?

A   Availability

B   Advocacy

C   Integrity

D   Insecurity

E   Contradictory

F   Confidentiality

204 One of the competitors to ICA Inc has recently suffered a serious cyber security breach, this has led to the board of ICA Inc to review their cyber security processes. They have decided that their current policies are insufficient and they could have easily been breached in the same way as their competitor.

The board have identified the NIST cybersecurity framework as a useful tool to help with the cyber risk management. Given the recent attack on their competitors they appreciate the data and information that they hold that is attractive to attackers, and they are aware of the ways in which their rivals were attacked, plus they have identified some other approaches that they could be susceptible to. Having understood this they have started to implement control that will help prevent the attacks. They are set up clear guidelines about how any breaches should be communicated and what should be done to get back to full operation as soon as possible through disaster recovery plans and business continuity plans.

Which ONE principle of the core have ICA not yet considered?

A   Identify

B   Protect

C   Detect

D   Recovery

E   Integrity

205 Cuckooland Plc has just entered into an arrangement to store confidential customer information using a third party cloud storage provider. The management are aware that this will impact its AICPA cyber security risk management report.

Which ONE of the following statements is correct?

A   It should be included in the managements description under the heading factors that have a significant effect on inherent cyber security risks.

B   It should be included in the managements assertion section of the report.

C   The management should not report on this, it is up to the practitioner to explain this in the practitioner's opinion section.

D   It should be included as part of their cyber security risk governance structure

E   It is relevant to the prepare a statement of applicability section of the report.

Section 2

ANSWERS TO OBJECTIVE TEST QUESTIONS

ENTERPRISE RISK

1 B

A full definition of risk should allow for both upside and downside aspects and incorporate the concepts of both probability and impact.

2 D

Risk management is the process of reducing the adverse consequences either by reducing the likelihood of an event or its impact.

3 B

Risk appetite is determined by risk attitude and risk capacity.

4 B

The four strategies in TARA are Transfer, Avoid, Reduce, Accept.

5

Pure risks	Speculative risks
The risk that a fire may destroy company assets	The risk that a foreign exchange rate may change
The risk that a customer goes out of business	The risk relating to the level of future profits
The risk that a virus is introduced to a computer application	The risk that a capital investment may not yield the predicted IRR

Note: Pure risks are only 'downside', whereas speculative risks may be 'upside' or 'downside'.

6   **The six steps in CIMA's risk management cycle are:**

Development of risk response strategy	3
Implement strategy and allocate responsibilities	4
Review and refine process and do it again	6
Identify risk areas	1
Implementation and monitoring of controls	5
Understand and assess scale of risk	2

7

Risk category	Risk
Business risks	Failure of a new product
Economic risks	Inflation rate rises
Environmental risks	Rate of climate change increases
Financial risks	Exchange rate changes

8

Risk category	Risk
Business risks	Raw material prices rise
Economic risks	Disposable income levels fall
Corporate reputation risks	CEO convicted of insider dealing
Political risks	Nationalisation of industry

9

Risk category	Risk
Political risks	Change of Government
Legal risks	Customer sues company for negligence
Regulatory risks	Government increases rate of Corporation Tax
Compliance risks	Company prosecuted for breach of the Data Protection Act

10   **A**

This is business risk, as it relates to the reputation of product(s), not the Company.

11   **B, C, E**

All the above are categories of risks. Gearing is included within financial risk and we are told that the company already look at this.

12   A, B, C

Viva Plc is financing the projects using debt therefore financial risk is critical to the success of the project as there is a risk the cost of debt could change and negatively impact the return of the project. As each casino is a multi-million pound project there is a risk that it may not deliver as planned and so there is a project risk. Viva operates all over the world so there will be a foreign exchange rate risk.

13   A, C

OKJ's risk analysis should focus on key high-impact, high-uncertainty factors in the organisation's environment.

A falls into this category – it is uncertain whether the government will put in place minimum wage legislation but this could have a significant impact on the company's profits. OKJ definitely needs a contingency plan for this.

B is relatively low impact (thanks to OKJ's insurance) and low uncertainty (OKJ seems confident that it will have to pay the fine), so no further analysis is needed.

C is another factor that is high impact (the cost of platinum rising sharply could cause a fall in profits) and high uncertainty (the movement in metal prices is uncertain, as is the likelihood of a recession). Again, OKJ may wish to consider contingency plans here – such as hedging against platinum price movements.

Finally D appears to be highly uncertain (it is not clear how long the CEO will stay with the company), but low impact (the remaining Board of Directors is capable of minimising disruption to the company), so again this is unlikely to be considered a high risk factor.

14

Term	Definition
risk capacity	'the amount of risk that the organisation is able to bear'
risk attitude	'the overall approach to risk'
risk appetite	'the amount of risk that the organisation is willing to accept in the pursuit of value added'

15   A, C, D

The number of directors is irrelevant. Although customers may have expectations regarding risk, this is not a direct determinant of risk appetite.

16   A

Although both SWOT and PEST(EL) analysis include external or environmental factors, they are used by managers INSIDE the organisation.

17

Risk Management Method		Strategy	
Transfer	2	Insurance transfers the risk to a third party	
Accept	1	The company has accepted that if it rains they will still hold the event	
Reduce	4	The use of internal controls will reduce the risks	
Avoid	3	This was considered dangerous so the company have avoided the risk	

18   6 (6MILLION, $6MILLION)

Once every five years is a probability of 20%. Simply multiply probability and impact to get expected value.

19   C

Political risk is the possibility of an unexpected politically motivated event in a country affecting the outcome of an investment. Political risk analysis will consider the differences between the home and target country, e.g. the stability of government, corruption by officials, different religious beliefs or ethnic tensions.

20   C

EV = 200 × 0.1 + 250 × 0.4 + 300 × 0.3 + 350 × 0.2 = 280

21   C

A risk attitude is one of either risk adverse or risk seeker here the managing director is risk adverse.

22   C, E

23   B

Particularly because it is a small consultancy firm, the death of the CEO would be high impact. However, unless there is a known condition, the probability of sudden death is low.

24   C

High staff turnover is common in the industry so probability is high.

Losing one sales person in a large organisation is unlikely to be anything other than low impact.

25   C

26   B

'Net risk' is calculated by multiplying probability and impact AFTER any action is taken to mitigate the risk.

27   A, C, D

A: It is possible that no further planning permission is granted in Country B without the payments.

B: The withdrawal of payments in Country B should have no effect on expansion in Country A since such payments have not been made there.

C: Managers may find it difficult to do their job without the authorisation to make additional payments, become dissatisfied and leave.

D: If expansion into Country B slows or stops overall performance is likely to be affected given that C Company only operates in one other location,

E: This is not a risk of not offering 'extra payments'.

28   B, C

A: This is not a risk to Q, rather a government risk.

B: The population of Q may be reluctant to purchase houses in a climate of interest rate rises despite government schemes.

C: If Q has taken out loans to fund expansion (for example to purchase new machinery) costs will increase.

D: The government are unlikely to withdraw schemes since their policy of encouraging people on to the housing ladder will not change.

E: The cost of land will not necessarily increase if interest rates go up, but if Q purchases land by taking out a loan then the costs of servicing the loan will go up.

29   A, D

A: It seems entirely reasonable to insure equipment but it is likely that internal controls over keeping it safe would also be required.

B: Increasing pay would probably not attract more staff since the scarcity seems to be caused by other factors and staff are already offered generous amounts.

C: It is unlikely that J can accept this. They will need to try and source supplies from alternative suppliers.

D: The 24hr support service is unpopular and is proving expensive with the court case.

30   B

The expected value criterion is independent of risk.

31

The expected value of purchases is:

	£
£400,000 × 0.3	120,000
£500,000 × 0.5	250,000
£600,000 × 0.2	120,000
	———
	490,000
	———

The volatility therefore is:

Downside (£600,000 – £490,000)	**£110,000**
Upside (£490,000 – £400,000)	**£90,000**

The volatility is the possible amount away from the expected value.

32   USD 707 MILLION

The Z value for a one-tail 95% confidence level is 1.645 (from the Normal Distribution tables).

VaR = standard deviation × Z value, so the

VaR = USD 430 million × 1.645 = 707.35 which rounds to 707.

33   C

Analysing the likelihood and impact is part of Risk Assessment.

34   A, B, C

35   A, B, E

COSO considers a WIDE range of risks, and is the responsibility of EVERYONE.

36   All answers are correct

Risk registers record pretty much everything relating to each risk identified

37   A, D, E

The 5 integrated elements are:

Control Environment, Risk assessment, control activities, information and communication and monitoring.

38   A

This is sometimes referred to as the 'tone at the top' of the organisation. It describes the ethics and culture of the organisation, which provide a framework within which each other aspect of internal control operate.

39   B

The Board of Directors are ultimately responsible for a company's system of internal controls.

40   A, C, E

41   B

X has bought a supplier, making it backward vertical integration.

42   A, B, C

These 3 are valid headings for a risk register.

D – is a general term relating to how much risk the business will accept.

E – is a general term relating to the maximum risk the business will accept.

43   D

You might want to argue that A, B or even C are commercially preferable to D. However, based on the information provided, there is a high likelihood of the Government of E acting in a way that would result in GS paying more tax then it would under option D.

44   D

The risk treatment for ISO31000 suggests seven ways an organisation may choose to deal with risk: avoiding the risk, accepting the risk, removing the risk source, changing the probability, changing the outcome, sharing the risk, retaining the risk.

45   D

A lack of consultation, concerns over patient care and a lack of a bonus all mean that surgeons are likely to ignore the new targets. The surgeons are unlikely to be demotivated by the target as internal targets are not their primary focus, patient care is.

46   A, D, E

A: If project managers were assessed on cost as well as successful completion of projects, this would probably lead to fewer external consultants being used.

B: The use of external consultants must be addressed rather than just the cost. This might improve the profit margins slightly but would not help to address the issue of use of external expertise instead of in house staff.

C: Presumably there are occasions where the use of external consultants is justified. The list will need to be retained for such situations. In addition, abolition of the list may lead to poor quality experts being used.

D: If senior management approval was required, project managers would think carefully before requesting external consultant help and unnecessary use of experts would not occur.

E: This would signal whether any particular managers overuse external experts. Such managers could be made aware of the issue.

47   A, B, D

Options A, B and D are not within Fred's control and so if his bonus depends on them he is likely to be demotivated.

Option C, E and F are potentially within Fred's control given the responsibility his employer gives him and so would motivate him to work harder and achieve his bonus.

48   A, B, D

Non-financial benefits include productivity, efficiency and satisfaction.

Expenditure is a financial measure.

49   A, C

There are several options which will reduce LAP's costs:

A – To avoid using freelancers more full-time staff should be employed. If there is a problem due to salary, then increase the salaries offered. This would still save on costs overall.

B – Overtime would not help if the skills are incorrect in the first place.

C – Full-time staff from other offices ($350) appears to be more expensive than using a freelancer ($300), however, the freelancer is an actual cost (or outflow of cash) whereas the internal recharge is not. Therefore, despite the higher cost of $350 LAP should use internal staff first.

D: Using freelancers 65% of the time = 65 × $300 = $19,500. Using full time staff = 100% × $150 = $15,000. It is cheaper to employ a full-timer overall.

50   B, C, F

The probability of a successful break in at the front is (0.05 × 0.1 × 0.15) × 100 = 0.075%

The probability of a successful break in at the rear is (0.1 × 0.15) × 100 = 1.5%

As it is front OR the rear, the overall probability of a successful break in is 1.5% + 0.075% = 1.575%

The rear has lower controls, making successful entry more likely.

STRATEGIC RISK

51   C, E

A fast changing environment increases the risk that long-term plans are out of date before they are implemented. Short term pressures from stakeholders (such as the need to pay a dividend) can make it difficult for a company to focus on long term plans.

However a formal planning process can appease banks which often prefer certain future plans and inexperienced managers are often better suited to formal planning that a more 'freewheeling' approach. Both differentiation and cost leadership strategies are compatible with long term planning.

52   B

If the currency of G-Land strengthens, its exports will become more expensive which will negatively impact its cost leadership strategy. Increasing demand elasticity would favour those who compete on price as this suggests consumers will be more affected by price than previously. Increased marketing costs are more likely to affect producers that compete by differentiating their products rather than by minimising prices. Investor focus on return on capital may discourage acquisition strategies but is unlikely to impact a choice between cost leadership and differentiation.

53   A, E

BVG's current generic strategy is one of differentiation so a proposal to expand into an industry in which cost leadership is seen as vital for survival, does not appear to be consistent. Competitors are less likely to react if an existing player is acquired as the overall market size (and so their effective share) remains unchanged.

Acquisition rather than organic growth would usually be seen as the best way to overcome barriers to entry. Due diligence appraisals are even more important when acquiring private companies as they are typically less well scrutinised. A resource based strategy is one which focuses on exploiting a company's core competencies – contrary to the expansion plan which will require BVG (a differentiator) to develop a core competence in cost leadership.

54   B, D

Disruptive innovation is the development of a brand new product which replaces rather than improves existing products. Products will usually be simple to use and when they are first introduced will be low cost (which is rarely compatible with high expenditure on research and development). Ease of distribution and accessibility will both enhance the chances of success.

55   C

Stress testing involves reviewing strategic decisions to evaluate how robust a business would be under pressure. Setting boundaries (such as limiting the product range) and clearly defining which stakeholders are prioritised (whether staff or shareholders) are both signs of a robust business. Encouraging competition would also be seen as a positive attribute as it helps to build creative tension. However a robust business would reduce its metrics to a small number of key variables to avoid management becoming conflicted over what to prioritise.

56   B, E

Reducing ward costs per patient or increasing beds occupied per day are both focused on improving efficiency (increasing the level of output for a given level of input). Aiming to reduce spending focuses on economy (bringing down the level of inputs into a process). Reducing waiting lists and improving patient outcomes are both focused on improving effectiveness (increasing outputs from a process).

57   A

Scenario planning involves imagining what alternative futures might look like and assessing possible course of action for chosen alternatives. Evaluation strategies and then implementing one is a form of long-term planning.   Reviewing priorities, flexibility, productivity and ways to measure performance is known as stress testing. Formulating a response on the basis of predicted competitor actions is using game theory. This might be used to develop a response to a given scenario during scenario planning.

58   A

Since BJK would prefer to operate independently, the options of joint venture and strategic alliance can be ruled out. Both would require the company to form partnerships with third party organisations. Since BJK does not have a particular wish to be involved in the marketing and sale of the product, the option of licensing, which would offer a licensee the right to exploit the product in return for a share of the proceeds, would be most appropriate. Franchising is more suitable for expanding a branded business model and requires the franchisor to provide support and a control framework for the franchisee.

59   C

Stress testing the current strategy to determine how robust it would be in uncertain times would be a logical approach for BHG. It would help to identify areas of weakness that might cause problems under pressure.

Scenario planning involves imagining what alternative futures might look like and assessing possible course of action for chosen alternatives. This is a costly and time-consuming process that is unlikely therefore to be suitable for a small and budget constrained company. BHG has a clearly defined differentiation strategy and therefore does not need to decide what its generic strategy should be. A company with a preference for gradual growth built on previous actions is unlikely to pursue a plan to develop disruptive innovation, although it is always possible that they may come across one unintentionally.

60   C

By focusing on building on its current reputation, FHY has adopted a 'resource-based' or 'competence-led' approach to strategic planning. A key risk with this approach is that a firm can lose sight of what customers want and overcomplicate the products it offers – thus a customer preference for simplicity is a particular risk factor.

Rapidly changing markets are a major problem for firms choosing a 'market-led' or 'positioning' approach (focused on identifying a suitable market position by analysing markets and competitors). A traditional approach (which starts with an examination of stakeholder objectives) can be problematic for firms with conflicting shareholder demands. Low cost producers are a threat for firms which try to sell on price. However, FHY is competing by differentiating itself from its competitors and thus is less at risk from their strategy.

61 A

Strengthening the company's internal control environment should minimise the opportunities for staff to commit fraud in the first place.

Paying a fair wage can help to reduce the motivation for employees to commit fraud. A fraud reporting system can discourage fraud and can also detect it should it still occur. Monitoring vacation balances can also help to detect fraud as employees may be reluctant to take holiday to avoid their actions being revealed.

62 B

One of the key factors in managing reputational risk is ensuring transparency in its communications with stakeholders. Preventing employees from discussing suppliers is likely to lead to accusations that FUO have something to hide, as is training the board to deflect queries from the media. Advertising messages are only likely to work if they can be shown to be backed up with action.

63 B, D, E

CSR involves aligning the company's core values with those of society – which the company must therefore understand. By developing an understanding of society's concerns BHY will be better able to anticipate the way in which legislation may develop. Metrics will need to be developed in order that progress towards the CSR goals can be assessed.

It is not necessarily true that costs will rise – many firms find that the new policies actually bring costs down. In addition, reputational improvements can strengthen sales and attract better staff. The needs of external stakeholders are not therefore necessarily being prioritised over those of shareholders – it can be profitable to be socially responsibility.

64 C

One of the most important aspects of reputational risk is losing the trust of stakeholders. Failing to offer explanations, failing to take action or failing to acknowledge responsibility for the problem are all strategies likely to destroy trust in the company.

BJI should therefore go public about the fault and immediately recall all the affected products.

65 A, B, C, D, E

Shareholders can dump shares driving down the share price. Customers can move their loyalty to SRT's competitors (and sue for damages resulting from the sale of faulty goods). Staff may not wish to be tainted with working for a company with a poor reputation and so leave SRT. Suppliers may fear that their own reputations could also become tarnished and so refuse to continue supplying the company. Investors may increase the cost of finance to reflect the increased risk they now perceive to be associated with SRT or refuse to offer further finance at all.

66 A, C, D

Sales staff at the SOs will be incentivised to offer a high part exchange value for old caravans as this will reduce the final cost to customers, encouraging them to buy expensive caravans and so increasing sales staff's bonuses.

BHP will want MD to transfer caravans to SO in Country B at a high transfer price. This will move profits from Country B to Country A which will then help to reduce the group's overall charge to tax.

BHP will wish to pay a low price to RHS. This will avoid high profits being earned by RHS company which would increase its charge to tax.

Minimising costs in RSC would be a benefit to SO as this would increase the overall value of second-hand caravan sales and so its overall revenue would be higher. However RSC is recompensed on a direct cost plus basis – this means that all their costs are recovered and there is no incentive to reduce the costs incurred.

67 B, D, E

Whilst a falling company share price or increasing employee turnover may indicate that the company's reputation is at risk, they do not provide specific information about where the problems lie. However customers' views (whether on-line or via direct discussion) and actions (such as returning the goods) provides a clear indication of reputational issues.

68 B, C, E

Reputational risk management is part of a business's long-term planning and should be built firmly into the corporate culture. Crisis management is a short-term response requiring specific planned actions (which will be regularly updated and tested) based on uncontrollable events. Both systems will be based on an assessment of the issues likely to affect the company.

69 A

Group companies that use transfer pricing techniques to artificially move profits from high tax regimes to low ones have come under media scrutiny and have suffered reputational damage. Maintaining goal congruence, providing companies with a degree of autonomy and recording transactions are considered to be appropriate uses of transfer pricing.

70 C, D, E

Whilst adopting a CSR framework may improve a company's brand, the implications are far more wide-ranging than just brand management, affecting factors such as company share price and profits, employee satisfaction and market opportunities. Effective CSR can also lower costs. The CSR work done by companies is therefore of direct interest to investors and all companies therefore need to report to stakeholders on CSR. The importance of CSR for a company's long-term future illustrates the importance of ensuring the engagement of senior staff.

71   A, B, E

C is an example of normal business practice.

D by definition of how an average is calculated, is also quite normal. Some organisation will pay above the average and some will pay below, an organisation that aims for cost leadership is likely to be below average.

The other options, even for an organisation pursuing cost leadership, would lead to negative coverage and damage to reputation.

72   D

MLC have clearly positioned themselves as an ethical company and will therefore attract shareholders who are looking for ethical investments and customers looking for ethically produced goods. If they continue trading with this supplier then their reputation will suffer if the news gets out. By taking strong decisive action and controlling the news story they have demonstrated that they follow their stated ethical principles.

73   B, D, E

A is incorrect, it is actually describing brand, reputation is harder to control than brand.

B is correct, it could have a negative impact on the local reputation of DMI. Litter and the environment is increasingly in the news and if DMI is perceived to be associated with it then it could lead to people going elsewhere for their pizza and ice cream.

C is incorrect, reputation risk is often linked to other forms of risk. For example a cyber-attack could lead to reputational damage, as could a legal case or fines for failing to comply with government legislation.

D is correct, although people are generally more concerned with the downside risk.

E is a correct description of reputation.

74   C

The basic principle here is that of confidentiality. To go outside of the business and professional environment in this manner without first considering the other options presented would not be following recommended process.

A – CIMA's ethics helpline exists to give members advice and is not a breach of confidentiality as it is within the professional arena. B – Reporting the company to the environment agency would comply with relevant legislation, however you would need to sure of your facts before whistle blowing. D – The Audit committee should be all NEDs and therefore a logical place to go, particularly as they are also responsible for the whistle blowing policy.

75   C, D, E

A strong CSR approach may, in fact, increase costs as the organisation has to source its goods more carefully. There is no reason why a strong CSR approach would speed up decision making in the organisation – in fact it is likely to use up management time that could be spent helping to earn the business higher profits. However, CSR often helps to attract both customers and staff, and reduces that chance that governments will be forced to regulate against unethical business behaviour in future.

76   A, C, D

A: Potential customers can easily switch as the market is competitive.

B: This seems unlikely given that HH sources clothes from many different suppliers.

C: This is a risk since the 'minimum standards' plan will cost money to devise and implement.

D: A recall is more ethical since if successful, it will prevent injury completely.

77   A, C, E

The code has five fundamental ethical principles. Integrity, Objectivity, Professional competence and due care, Confidentiality and Professional behaviour.

78   B, C, E

These are the three major reasons for disclosure of confidential information to third parties.

79   A

Integrity would be compromised as finance professionals should be straightforward and honest.

80   B

Objectivity would be compromised due to the conflict of interest this situation presents.

81   C

CPD is needed to maintain professional competence.

82   D

Divulging the details requested would breach confidentiality.

83

Refuse to remain associated with the conflict	4
Check the facts	1
Escalate externally	3
Escalate internally	2

84   A

John can ultimately benefit financially from his actions so his objectivity may be compromised.

85   C

Gemma is being asked to promote a position or opinion to the point that subsequent objectivity may be compromised.

86   A, B, E

A: Integrity implies that a person should be straightforward and honest in all business relationships. The management accountant is not being honest because the budgets produced are known to be inaccurate.

B: Objectivity: By taking the tickets to a major event in exchange for altering figures the management accountant is allowing bias to override business judgements.

C: The management accountant's skills are not under question and so this principle does not appear to have been breached.

D: The management accountant does not appear to have breached confidentiality. The conversations Stephanie overheard involved Alpha staff and so no information has been leaked.

E: The management accountant has not behaved professionally and in line with expectations of a CIMA® member. In addition to using incorrect figures in the budgets there has been an attempt to influence Stephanie to do the same.

87   A, B, D

A – Travel Co may feel that by apologising potential customers might feel they were at fault. Legally they had a contract saying that the rooms should be safe and the manager signed it, thus passing the responsibility to the manager. However, morally Travel Co should accept some blame since they didn't check whether the manager had made the rooms safe.

B and C – Travel Co has not explained why it has chosen to award only $350,000 of the $3 million to the family. The sum seems quite small in comparison, but how much is a life worth? The question to many people will be irrelevant. The morally right thing to do would be to give the family the full $3 million (or more). It is potentially a small sum in comparison to their profits and would go a long way to repairing their reputation. Travel Co's share price has fallen considerably demonstrating the public's feelings for their actions.

D – Travel Co should investigate every room if possible but this would increase Travel Co's costs which would ultimately be passed on to their customers. In each hotel there could be hundreds of rooms and Travel Co may contract with thousands of hotels. It might be more cost efficient to issue strict guidelines on the safety of rooms and ensure they have a tight contract with each hotel. Then they might sample check rooms. The news of the deaths should ensure that most hotel owners will check their own hotels since it is their reputation that will be harmed.

E – The publicity that Travel Co has received has not been good and the falling share price demonstrates that not all advertising is good for the company. Sales will potentially fall in future seasons unless Travel Co makes amends.

88   A, C, D

A – Integrity implies fair dealing and truthfulness. Catalina does not meet this criterion as she lied to the council about still being the owner of the business.

B – Objectivity means that Catalina should not allow bias or a conflict of interest in business judgements.

C – Confidentiality – The trainee stole the client details and used them to disparage the business. Therefore this ethical principle was not met. Catalina should have kept the client details secure.

D – Professional behaviour – Catalina has closed the business bank account and changed her telephone number. She does not appear to want to return the $350 rent which she owes. This is theft and not in keeping with being a CIMA® member.

E – Professional competence and due care – Catalina's professional knowledge and skill is not in question. It is her behaviour that is questionable.

89   D

Answer D is not a benefit of corporate governance since corporate governance is the set of processes and policies by which the company is directed, administered and controlled and will therefore not prevent fraudulent claims by an external party, i.e. contractors.

Answer A is a benefit since good governance will result in a better image with the providers of finance thus making raising finance easier.

Answer B is also a benefit since good governance should result in sustainable wealth creation.

Answer C is a benefit since customers will prefer to purchase a product or service from a company that has a strong reputation for good governance and hence lower levels of risk.

90   D

Directors are placed in control of resources which they do not own and are effectively agents of the shareholders. They should be working in the best interests of the shareholders. However, they may be tempted to act in their own interests, for example by voting themselves huge salaries. The background to the agency problem is the separation of ownership and control – in many large companies the people who own the company (the shareholders) are not the same people as those who control the company (the board of directors).

91   D

External audit is planned by the external auditor. Processing of journals is an operational role and should therefore not be performed by internal audit.

92   B

Chair and CEO are the two key roles in the organisation and therefore should be held by separate people to dilute power.

93   C, D

94   A, B, C

95   B, C, D

The remuneration committee should consist of independent NED's only and should not consider NED remuneration. This should be decided by the board as a whole and/or shareholders depending on the specific requirements in the company Articles of Association.

96   B

Non-executive directors are required for a balanced board. A chair needs to be appointed so the roles of chair and chief executive can be separate.

97   B

Non-executive directors do not take part in the routine executive management of a company, but must participate at board meetings.

98   C

Whilst the best trigger for the awarding of a bonus would be the director achieving a range of individual performance targets, share options would best align remuneration to shareholder interests as both parties would want the company share price to rise to maximise their individual financial return.

99   B, C, E

A: NED's do not directly set strategies since they have no operational responsibilities. Despite the NED's in the question possibly having the direct experience to enable them to set strategy, this is not their role in governance.

B: Scrutiny of decisions made by the board on behalf of the shareholders is one of the main roles of NED's.

C: Similarly risk monitoring is a role of NED's.

D: External analysis is part of strategy setting and so falls to the executive board to carry out. NED's would be expected to question external analysis but not carry it out in the first instance.

E: The nominations committee is majority NED and would be involved here.

100   A, C

A: The presence of such a senior director would ensure the actions of the chair/CEO were questioned and he/she/they would be held to account. This would make unfettered power less likely and the combined role less risky.

B: This argument suggests the combined role is too great for one individual and so supports a split.

C: This argument suggests that splitting the role will not lead to good governance or guard against corporate failure.

D: If a combined CEO and chair will be more expensive than a single CEO this is unlikely to be an argument to keep a unified structure.

E: This is a clear argument for splitting the roles.

101 C, D, E

A is incorrect as she is related to the marketing director, she is not independent.

B is not correct because she is not independent, according the corporate governance code the audit committee must be made up entirely of INEDs

C is true, because she is not independent, according the corporate governance code the audit committee must be made up entirely of INEDs

D is true because of her lack of independence, she should not be deciding her father's pay.

E is true, it is unlikely that someone in their first full time job, who has just completed studying is experienced enough to be on the board.

F is incorrect. There are no pre requisites for time served at a company to join the board. Only that to be independent a director cannot have worked at the company within the last five years.

G is not correct. There are no pre requisites for qualifications to join a board. Only that one person on the audit committee has recent and relevant financial experience.

INTERNAL CONTROLS

102

Category	Example
Financial	Variance analysis
	Reviewing aged debt listing
Quantitative	Customer satisfaction score
	Absenteeism rate
Qualitative	Employee training
	Organisational structure

Financial controls express financial targets and spending limits and include budgetary control (e.g. variance analysis) and controls over sales, purchases, payroll and inventory cycles (like an aged debt review).

Non-financial quantitative controls focus on targets against which performance can be measured and monitored. Examples include balanced scorecard targets such as customer satisfaction scores or absenteeism rates.

Non-financial qualitative controls form the day-to-day controls over most employees in organisations. Examples include employee training and management control methods such as organisational structure.

103

Category	Example
Financial	Bank reconciliations
	Budgetary controls
Quantitative	Number of defects
	Number of new products launched
Qualitative	Lock on a store room door
	Contract of employment

Non-financial quantitative controls as well as the balanced scorecard (innovation – number of new products launched) can also include TQM quality measures such as number of defects.

Non-financial qualitative controls also include physical controls such as locks on a door as well as management controls such as contracts of employment.

For more detail see also the explanation for 102.

104

Control environment	Risk assessment
The organisation shows a commitment to ethical values	Clear objectives to allow risk identification and assessment
Accountability of employees for their areas of responsibility	That risk identification and analysis does take place across the entity
Human resource policies and practices to help attract, develop and retain suitable talent	The potential for fraud arising in pursuit of the stated objectives must be considered
	The internal controls system must be reviewed for changes in the external environment

105 A

B will not help improve quality itself and therefore does not link to the CSF identified.

C is not specific – how will the company decide if 'quality' is improved by 50%?

D has no measurable target for the amount of training that will be undertaken.

106 C

By definition.

107

Internal Control		Risk
A	Prepare and reconcile budget to actual spend	1
B	Hedging techniques	4
C	Tight stock control systems	3
D	CCTV cameras in store	2

108 B

2 is an objective of the purchase cycle. 4 is an objective of the payroll cycle.

109 D

1 and 2 are objectives of the purchase cycle.

110 B

1 prevents stock-outs/manufacturing delays. 4 prevents unnecessary goods being ordered.

111 B

2 prevents stock-outs/manufacturing delays. 3 gives assurance about the quality of goods and reliability of supply.

112 B, C

A – Increased training is more likely to increase the rejection rate.

D – Inspections occur before goods get to finished goods inventory.

E – Employing more quality inspectors is more likely to increase the rejection rate.

113 A, B, D

C – Reducing inventory levels may reduce how much thieves can steal but not the number of thefts.

E – Trying to pass the buck to suppliers is unlikely to affect thefts in X's stores.

114 A, B, E

A: If examiners receive more standard training they are likely to behave in a more standardised way, in accordance with the training received.

B: This will reduce the chance of a test centre being accused of being strict or lenient because of its staff.

C and D will not reassure drivers on the test.

E: Should convince learners that they are tested in the same way and to the same standards wherever they take the test.

F: This will not reassure drivers the test is the same, it will just prevent the variations in pass rates seen in the question.

115 B, C

A: Whilst holding more oil would prevent reoccurrence of the late delivery (caused by a stock out), it would increase rather than decrease liquidity risk.

B: This would take the element of judgement away from the inventory manager and ensure that a certain amount of stock was always on hand. Provided this level was set correctly, it should prevent reoccurrence of the problem.

C: If the supplier could reduce lead times it may prevent a stock out but not affect liquidity.

D: This may help with the liquidity problems but not the stock holding costs. In addition, the supplier will be even less inclined to deliver quickly if payment is withheld or delayed.

E: A new supplier of oil would likely bring with it the same issues as G has currently and in addition they are scarce so a new supplier may charge more or be difficult to find.

116 A, D

A: This should reduce the risk of maintenance work being paid for without a record of which flat it relates to. If H has a record of which flat the work relates to, the costs can be recharged.

B: This will help to make sure that invoices are not paid unless work has been done or goods received but will not help H to know which flat the invoice relates to.

C: This may help H to recover more costs than at present but will not reduce the risk of costs not being correctly recharged to flat owners. Some flats with lots of miscellaneous items may not be charged enough and others may be charged too much.

D: This will ensure no invoices are missed and all are recharged.

E: This may ensure all costs are recharged but not correctly to flat owners.

117 A, B, C

A: Q may need to source contractors from outside the local area which is likely to increase costs.

B: Unless Q pays for the insurance which seems unlikely this will be the case.

C: Since local contractors are unlikely to have the accreditation, there will be a shortage and work will back up.

D: There does not appear to be a problem with Q getting the insurance but paying for it seems difficult.

E: This does not appear to be a problem for Q.

118 C

Range checks can help ensure completeness but not security.

119 C

Counterfeiting is a criminal offence and the company may also incur liability for the tort of passing off.

120 A

It would appear that there is no control environment within the company.

121 D

The lack of controls have created an opportunity.

122 B

'Fraud risk is one component of operational risk. Operational risk focuses on the risks associated with errors or events in transaction processing or other business operations. A fraud risk review considers whether these errors or events could be the result of a deliberate act designed to benefit the perpetrator.'

(Taken from the CIMA publication 'Fraud risk management – A guide to good practice')

123 A, B, C

An effective anti-fraud strategy has four main components – prevention, detection, deterrence and response.

(Taken from the CIMA publication 'Fraud risk management – A guide to good practice')

124 A, B, D

CIMA recommends that organisations have:

- a mission statement that refers to quality or, more unusually, to ethics and defines how the organization wants to be regarded externally

- clear policy statements on business ethics and anti-fraud, with explanations about acceptable behaviour in risk prone circumstances

- a route through which suspected fraud can be reported

- a process of reminders about ethical and fraud policies – e.g. annual letter and/or declarations

- an aggressive audit process that concentrates on areas of risk

- management who are seen to be committed through their actions.

(Taken from the CIMA publication 'Fraud risk management – A guide to good practice')

125 A

126 A, B, C

CCTV could help reduce the inventory discrepancies, segregation of duties should help the bank reconciliation and controls over the use of USB drives could help reduce the incidents of leaked information.

Calling the NCA is more of a response that would be used if significant thefts were taking place, at this stage increased controls would be more appropriate to help reduce the opportunity and motive.

127   B, D, E

A and C would not reduce the number of attacks, but would help with the response to an attack.

B would reduce the amount of time a staff member is walking on their own and so should reduce the opportunity for an attack to occur.

D, while it would be impossible to have all staff end their shift in daylight hours, particularly during winter, if they can reduce the proportion of staff finishing work in the dark it would reduce the opportunity for attacks.

E, while we do not know where attacks occur, it would reduce the likelihood of an attack in these areas and should therefore reduce the numbers of attacks overall.

128   C

One of the fraud alerts is unusual, irrational or inconsistent behaviour such as employees who arrive first and leave last in the evening and do not take time off. The theory is this gives them opportunity to perpetrate the fraud while no-one else is around and by never taking time off they can avoid anyone else doing their work and noticing any discrepancies. This makes JX most likely to have committed the fraud.

The other 3 options have either been under close supervision or had significant time off during the period of time when the fraud has been occurring.

129   C

Management authorisation will decrease the chances of fraudulent and inaccurate payments being made to non-existent payables.

False billing scams are where companies are sent fraudulent invoices with the hope that some will pay them. Segregation of duties (A) will not prevent such invoices being received. Similarly, neither regular reconciliations between ledgers (B), nor maintaining a trial balance (D) will not identify that the invoices are false. The only way of doing this is to ensure all invoices are authorised as valid before payment.

130   A, C, D

B will not restore shareholder confidence.

E will please shareholders but do nothing about their confidence that similar frauds will not happen again.

F is unfair to the staff concerned who should not be dismissed without following due process and without good reason.

131   A, B

A: This is definitely a key consideration. The potential cost of reputation risk is high and would far outweigh and cost savings from reduced inspections.

B: Maintenance staff may not do checks as rigorously on the segments and may be less likely to pick up issues.

C: Reporting to management will still take place weekly but be less extensive.

D: Controls should represent value for money (and cost benefit analysis should be carried out), however low cost should not be the overriding priority rather effectiveness.

E: Corrosion checks are internal controls in response to evolving risks and so are relevant to risk assessment.

132 B, C, D

A: Will not prevent theft of finished goods inventory since it relates to raw materials and whether orders are correctly received.

B: Will provide protection from theft by unauthorised access.

C: Will allow R Co to detect fraudulent claims relating to employment history.

D: Will help prevent IT security breaches.

E: Will not help to prevent theft but may assist with rework costs and customer satisfaction.

133 A, C

A: Potential customers unable to enter the car park are likely to park somewhere else leading to a direct loss of revenue.

B: The ticket machines can take payment without issuing a receipt therefore no revenue will be lost.

C: Lack of segregation of duties could lead to potential for fraud.

D, E and F: These are not control weaknesses.

134 A, B, D

135 A, B, D, E

136

Internal Audit	External Audit
Required by shareholders	Required by statute
Reports to Audit Committee or Directors	Reports to Shareholders and Management
Reports on controls	Reports on financial statements

137

Suggestion	Internal Audit Attribute Standard contravened
Jan, as Head of Internal Audit, should report to the Finance Director	Independence
the first project for the new department should be to audit the Treasury Department, which Jan currently manages	Objectivity
It should not be a problem that Jan has no experience of audit and is only part-qualified.	Professional Care
	None contravened

138 D

Finance staff should not be involved with internal audit work. To ensure errors are identified, someone other than the preparer should review the work.

139 **Gap 1 – C (competitive), gap 2 – B (internal), gap 3 – A (process)**

Competitive benchmarking is likely to help identify risk areas where the firm is performing much worse (or better) than rivals, but it can be difficult to convince a successful rival to share their secrets. As internal benchmarking focuses on other parts of the same organisation, this type of benchmarking often fails to provide insight into performance compared with rivals but can identify under-performing divisions, for example. Process benchmarking can be difficult as there may be few, if any, non-competing businesses that have the same core processes as our organisation. It is therefore often undertaken for non-core activities.

140 **A**

Ratio analysis is one type of analytical procedure. An analytical procedure requires evaluation of plausible relationships between financial and non-financial information. Inspection, observation and enquiry are different types of auditing techniques.

141 **C**

1 is incorrect since internal audit would not retain their independence if they reviewed an area for which they had operational responsibility.

3 is incorrect since internal audit would not retain their independence if they implemented controls, their role is to review the controls once implemented.

2 is correct as ISA 610 allows the auditors to obtain direct assistance from internal auditors under supervision of the audit firm.

142 **C, D, E**

A – family run companies do not necessarily have weaker controls or higher risks.

B – just because the company is a plc, it does not necessarily follow that it is listed.

F – while one would hope the shareholders would want an internal audit department, this reason is not as important as the other factors highlighted.

143 **A, B, C, D**

A – compliance audits check the implementation of rules, regulations and procedures. Checking other stores implementation of the discounting policy would be applicable at B retail.

B – a management audit aims to identify existing and potential management weaknesses. Auditor may want to judge whether poor management/staff relations for instance may have led to the breaches in procedure.

C – a systems audit would be appropriate: it would examine the objective of discounting stock, how the procedure works and what the current controls are, other ways to manage discounting etc. The entire process of discounting could be reviewed rather than just whether the current policy is being breached elsewhere. It may be the policy is out of date or the EPOS system can easily be overridden.

D – risk based auditing can be applied in this scenario. It may be the breaches occurred in stores that shared staff or where small stores where it may be more difficult to oversee and supervise staff. Audit may therefore choose to focus on such stores as a priority.

E – environmental auditing is concerned with ensuring environmental safeguarding policies and regulations are being met. This is not applicable in this scenario.

144 D

A systems-based audit is an audit of the internal controls within an organisation. The term can refer to any type of system.

145 A, B, C, D, E

All of the above may apply. Depending on the audit, certain sections may go into more depth.

146 A, B, C

A: This is a key reason why companies outsource internal audit or recruit from outside. Internal candidates can be too close to the organisation to view it objectively.

B: External recruits will not have carried out work in any other role at BGT so this is not a risk.

C: Is another key reason to recruit externally.

D and E are not necessarily the case. Internal recruits may have skills which are more specific and helpful to BGT and internal promotion may be very slow given the concerns over lack of candidates.

147 A, B

A: The presence of an internal auditor checking the robustness of internal controls can act as deterrent although this is not its primary purpose.

B: Z could make suggestions for improvements but the implementation of such suggestions would be management's responsibility.

C: Internal auditors should not have operational responsibility.

D: Z would only investigate fraud if management asked them to do so. If management were unaware of the fraud then this would not be possible.

E: Again, Z could have only done this at the request of management.

148 B, C, E

A: Internal audit do not carry out any operational work and so would not manage the sales function. Rather, as presented in Option 3 they would oversee the systems changeover and ensure controls are adequate.

B: Investors prefer to see a well monitored company as it reassures them their investment is safe.

C: See comments on Option 1.

D: Best practice dictates that an organisation should review the need for internal audit at regular intervals so not replacing the IA was not a direct contravention.

E: This is a main argument for establishing internal audit.

149 **A, C, E**

A: This is good practice and should happen, it should reduce the managers concerns as they will be made aware of the contents of the report before anyone else.

B: This should not be true as it would bring into question the independence of the report, although it would help reduce the managers concerns if it were true.

C: This would be part of best practice, and the fact that the report remains a confidential document should help reduce the managers concerns about their reputation.

D: This is true of best practice, but it wouldn't reduce the managers concerns about reputation and opportunity to respond.

E: This is part of best practice and would also help reduce the managers concerns about not having an opportunity to respond.

CYBER RISKS

150 **A, B, E**

The main types are personal, business and classified.

Secret recipes and employee information are specific examples of business information and personal information respectively.

151 **A, B, D, F**

The six principles are reciprocity, scarcity, authority, consistency, liking and consensus.

152 **D**

It appears the manager has clicked on a link in a phishing email.

Keylogging is a form of spyware, botnets are a network of private computers infected with malware and controlled as a group without the owners' realising, often associated with a distributed denial of service attack where multiple computers overwhelm a system with requests. Screenshotting is not a type of attack.

153 **C**

If financial data is improperly modified, the cyber security objective 'integrity of data' is threatened. This objective relates to guarding information held by the organisation against unauthorised interference.

The objective of 'availability' relates to ensuring access to information and systems, 'confidentiality' relates to preventing unauthorised disclosure of information, and 'integrity of processing' relates to protecting the information systems from improper interference.

154 **A, E**

Personal information is anything that on its own, or when combined with other information, can be used to identify, contact or locate a single person. Such information would include the addresses of nominated recipients and the contents of message cards which may include names, dates of birth etc.

Product specifications, sales forecasts and feedback scores would be classed as Business Information.

155 C

The external call centre is a service provider which expands BBJ's network and so increases its cybersecurity risk.

156 B, D, E

Acquiring a new facility will involve expanding the company's network. Outsourcing the Human Resources department will mean facilitating external access to employee data. Replacing laptops will require secure disposal of the old machines (the new machines may well improve cyber-security if they run better protection software).

Changing the specification of a product and revaluing assets both involve altering information held by the company but not the potential access to it.

157 D

The link between the inventory store and the component suppliers expands FFK's network and so exposes them to a cyber-security threat. Phone orders are a potential business risk but not a cyber-security threat.

158 A, D, E

A company page on a social media site would help BKL to promote awareness of the company and provide customers with a forum to provide feedback. However if the page is not updated for new products / discontinued products etc. this could damage the reputation of the company.

Whilst social media can be used to screen potential job candidates, this involves reviewing their social media sites not setting up a company specific one. DoS attacks are ones that overwhelm the company's own system resources but holding an information page on a social media site would not of itself increase BKL's vulnerability to such an attack.

A DoS attack could of course be launched on the social media site but the effect on BKL would be lack of customer access to its page rather than an overwhelmed system.

159 A, D

This is an example of an SQL injection attack which occurs when the attacker is able to inject code into an input box on a company's website (here an unprotected password box) which then sends a request to the database supporting the website. The attacker was then able to download information from the database. The hacker used the attack to steal customer addresses which are a form of Personal Information and can be used to help identify the customer.

The use of an external delivery company is not here being exploited although it could of course increase the company's risk of other types of cyber-attacks. Spear Phishing is where a specific individual is targeted using fraudulent messages to access sensitive information. Malvertising is where advertisements appearing on a company's webpages are maliciously infected with malware which can affect every visitor to that page.

160 A, C, D

Training and passwords do not mitigate risk in the development process.

161 A

If the website crashed it would be unavailable and prevent customers from placing their order.

162 A, B, D

Pilot changeover cannot be used, as it assumes that any 'lessons learned' in the first changeover can be transferred to all of the other sites. Given each site uses different systems currently it would be difficult to transfer lessons learnt at one site.

163 A, B, D, E

Confidentiality of PII held on a tablet is a cyber risk, as is the security of a tablet, disruption to communication systems is also a cyber risk. A DDoS attack using botnets is a form of application attack.

A competitor advertising online to gain market share is a business risk.

164 A, B, D

An acquisition of a competitor is likely to lead to several IT challenges as systems are integrated, any change like this could lead to increased opportunities for unauthorised access.

A significant change in organisational restructure is likely to change reporting lines, and user access requirements, this leads to potential cyber risks through inappropriate access to information or systems.

The local market trader has not had any significant change to operations, just effectively opening for longer hours.

The window cleaner has increased their usage of IT, they have potentially gone from very low likelihood of cyber security issues to significant risks relating to customers personal data.

Changing the culture of an organisation does not necessarily lead to a change in the cyber security risk management.

165 A, D

Testing reduces the probability of failure, and data backup reduces the impact.

166 B, C, D

EU Member States can introduce exemptions from the GDPR's transparency obligations and individual rights, but only where the restriction respects the essence of the individual's fundamental rights and freedoms and is a necessary and proportionate measure in a democratic society to safeguard things like national security and breaches of ethics in regulated professions.

167 C, D

Ransomware and Trojans are forms of malware, ethical hacking is done to help an organisation, usually at the organisations request.

168 A, B, C

Expansion is into a new country is a significant change and will impact the cyber risk profile of FF.

Offering a software application that can take payments and processes personal data will impact the cyber risks of FF.

PII is anything that can be used either on its own or with other information to identify, contact or locate a single person, so all of the basic data mentioned fits that description.

People could still post damaging reviews on social media rather than the app and so it must still be monitored.

Integrity of data relates to making sure that the information is reliable and remains up to date, so FF still need to have procedures in place to make sure that the data remains up to date.

As one of the objectives of GDPR is the protection of the principle of free movement of personal data within the EU, they are operating in the EU country of Ukland so will need to comply.

169 C

SQL injection attacks occur when the attacker uses an unprotected input box on the target company's website to execute a SQL query to the database via the input data from the client to server. A successful SQL injection can read sensitive data from the company's database, modify (insert, update or delete) database data, execute administration operations (such as shutdown) on the database, recover the content of a given file, and, in some cases, issue commands to the operating system.

170 E

The dark web is the part of the internet that allows increased anonymity and is the most common place for cyber criminals to sell PII.

The tor browser or tor network is one of the well-known ways to access the dark web. The surface web is the part of the internet used every day and searchable via search engines. The deep web is accessible through a login credential and an example would be your online bank account. The sinister web does not exist.

171 A

Polymorphic malware is a type of malware that avoids being identified by systems and networks by constantly changing its identifiable features, the idea being the longer it remains undetected on a system, network or device the more data it can steal.

A type of malware that records every keystroke typed by the victim is a keylogger.

An issue within some software that is known to the developer but has been left unaddressed is known as a zero day exploit or vulnerability.

A type of malware that specifically targets the banking industry due to a banks perceived attractiveness for attack from criminals is a banking Trojan, although, these can now be used against other attractive industries.

172 B

This is a description of Business Email Compromise.

173 B, C

Social engineering is used because cyber defences are becoming increasingly difficult to breach, but the human element is more susceptible through either carelessness (potentially when rushing) and because they often don't see themselves as part of the defence against a cyber-attack.

Social engineering is therefore very relevant to cyber crime and cyber security.

Ethical hackers help organisations defend against a cyber-attack. Weaponised documents do work, but they often need an individual to allow them onto the network or system by downloading or opening a document.

174 B

Network configuration management is the practice of organising and maintaining information about all the different elements in a computer network such as locations, IP address, default settings, versions of software installed etc. This would allow CXD to monitor configuration changes and compliance with software updates.

It is blockchain systems that prevent data modification without the consent of all participants in the network. Security information and event management (SIEM) can analyse patterns in system data.

175 A, B, D, E

All staff using the same password would be poor IT policy and increase the likelihood of both internal and external issues. Allowing staff absolute freedom on social media could increase cyber risks through clicking on malicious links or potential spearphishing from hackers.

The rest are sensible precautions to help reduce the cyber risk an organisation faces.

176 A

All of the actions described demonstrate good cyber-security management. However disaster recovery refers to the ability to restore data and applications that run a business should if some part of the infrastructure gets damaged or destroyed – which cloud based data back-up will provide.

Anti-virus software, centralised monitoring and SSL certificates are all designed to avoid a disaster occurring in the first place.

177 A

User-names and access codes help to identify who has accessed or modified the system. Passwords or PINs help with authentication – i.e. they provide confidence that the person accessing the system matchings the identification used.

Use of SSL certification is a sophisticated form of digital authentication.

Authorisation limits what parts of a system can be accessed.

178 C, D, E

Variety is important and as all the letter are uppercase, changing some to lowercase would improve it. The password is more than 8 characters and so is of reasonable length. The password does seem to be significant to JR, their place of work and potentially JR's year of birth, if this is the case it could be more easily guessed.

JR should not share their password with anyone and should not write it down.

179 A

Monitoring ISO27001 compliance, ensuring business continuity and maintaining back-up (hot) sites may all fall within the remit of an SOC, but its overall objective is far broader – to monitor, assess and defend systems and respond to threats as necessary.

180 D

Creating a strong password that is difficult to guess is good general advice about passwords.

The rest are examples of bad password uses.

181 C

Endpoint security refers to how an organisation protects its network when it is accessed via remote devices such as laptops or mobile phones.

182 D

Examples of back-ups that organisations now use are mirror sites, hot back up site, warm back up site and cold back up site.

A buffer overflow is a type of application attack.

183 D

Encryption of data involves scrambling the contents in such a way that only authorised recipients can unscramble and access it.

The other approaches are sensible cyber security policies, but not specific to the transmission of confidential information to a third party.

184 B, C

As Montyrubble is expanding into B2B sales some organisations only partner with ISO27001 compliant suppliers, it helps reduce their cyber risks as they know the supplier is taking a proactive stance against cyber risks.

The IT manager is likely to already be quite busy with the proposed expansion into B2B. Chocolatiers are not known to be particularly susceptible to cyber risks. Being ISO27001 compliant cannot eliminate cyber risk completely so they will still need to be aware of cyber risks.

185 A, B, D, E

USB drives represent an additional endpoint on a network so increase cyber risk. Malware from the device is one of the risks, antivirus software could help with this, but may not be able to prevent all malware. Employees could transfer sensitive data onto the USB drives for work reasons and lose them, or they could steal sensitive information on a USB drive.

There are controls, such as encryption, that could help reduce the threat from information theft, banning their use is also a control.

186 C

Reverse engineering malware allows specialists to identify the point where it infiltrated the system and so patch the weak point.

Penetration testing would help BKL to identify where future malware could enter the system and identifying all the devices connected to the network could assist them in determining where endpoint security needs to be strengthened. Blockchain systems are often introduced as a way of protecting the system against future malware attacks.

187 A, B, C, D, E

Cyber security should be an enterprise wide activity, involving all staff from board level down to junior operational staff.

188 B, C

Web application tests would look at security surrounding applications such as payment systems, internal network testing considers vulnerabilities that could be exploited by a rogue internal user.

Infrastructure testing looks at the points where the system connects with the internet, wireless network tests look at access points and devices connected to the network, and simulated phishing tests assess the susceptibility of employees to breaching cyber security protocols.

189 B

Although the recovery process can be complex, a forensic examination of the data stored by the system should identify whether deleted material is still accessible.

190 B, C, E

A system level analysis is designed to identify changes that the malware has made – including changes to the operating system components and its configuration and the setting up of fake accounts.

It would be during a more detailed malware analysis that the company would hope to discover details of what the malware was designed for and how it infiltrated the system.

191 A, E

Penetration testing involves the use of ethical hackers (employees of Vera Inc), but if any of these are selling information on to third parties with malicious intent this could ruin Vera's reputation.

Employee training, certification and antivirus software are all types of protection Vera could sell.

Vera cannot completely prevent cyber attacks, but there work will make cyber breaches less likely to occur. Vera themselves are potentially more likely to be attacked as the motivation for some hackers is the thrill of the challenge and if they could breach Vera's system they could potentially gain access to all their clients systems too. Blockchain is not a specialised response to a cyber attack.

192 C, D

Antivirus and network configuration management are both useful tools to help protect against cyber risks.

Training is also useful, but the staff need to be vigilant for emails that look like they are from someone they trust but are not. A disgruntled employee can often pose a significant cyber risk to a firm and monitoring network traffic can help identify a known type of attack.

193 B, C, E

Network configuration management including segmenting the network can make it harder for anyone to gain unauthorised access to sensitive information. The type of penetration testing described is called internal network penetration testing. Basic business process controls are as important as IT and cyber security controls in protecting an organisation from cyber risks.

The need for security processes is increasing, and a Plc is likely to have significant sensitive information that is worth having. The internet of things is not limited to home devices and can be used in business too, often significantly increasing the number of access points to the organisations network.

194 A

Web application penetration testing would test for unprotected input boxes like this and so reduce the likelihood of an attacker being able to carry out such an attack.

Unethical hackers have malicious intent, an ethical hacker would be hired to carry out penetration testing. This type of attack was not due to staff clicking on inappropriate links, so while this training is sensible it wouldn't reduce the likelihood of this type of attack. BCP looks at responses and so would not reduce the likelihood of an attack in future, the attack did not stem from a BYOD, so a policy change would not impact the likelihood of a future SQL injection attack.

195   C

Storage analysis will help them identify if the files still exist on the compromised servers and if they were recoverable.

Reverse engineering is part of malware analysis. System level analysis helps identify what, if any changes have been made to the system, for example allowing the attacker to get back in without authorisation in the future. Network analysis monitors the amount of data on a network and can help identify the pattern of data flow in the lead up to the attack so that a similar attack could be spotted and prevented earlier.

196   A, C, E

The AICPA 2017 cyber security risk management reporting framework requires the reporting of relevant and useful information to stakeholders, which includes the requirement to consider materiality.

Attempted attacks on the company would be relevant to the stakeholder and should be reported – including the data under threat, the work done to fix the issue and any changes to security procedures as a result. A report into the company's cyber vulnerability is clearly directly relevant to stakeholders as is a decision to move to external providers with its associated expansion of HLP's network and risk to Personal Information held.

However, HLP is an international company and materiality considerations would therefore preclude the provision of minor details such as specific work done to the system or the number of software licenses held.

197   C

Customers will be providing PAR Company with Personal Information when transacting with the company and will be most concerned about ensuring that it remains confidential.

198   C

The company's risk governance structure should include processes to support the functioning of the cybersecurity risk management program, such as meetings with the company board.

Expanding the network would be included as a 'change that could affect cyber security risk', insurance falls under 'risk assessment procedures' and measures to prevent unauthorised access are 'control processes'.

199   B

The use of an external service provider must be included in the section 'Factors affecting inherent cyber security risks. The other sections require general descriptions of company policies but need not necessarily describe the detailed arrangements entered into with a specific service provider.

200   B

The AICPA recommends that a certified public accountant should be appointed to provide the required opinion.

201   B, C, E

The purpose of the frameworks is to give organisations guidance how to prepare for, prevent, detect and respond to a cyber attack. This means A and D are incorrect.

As with most risks, cyber risks are changing all the time, so they cannot eliminate the risk of cyber attack completely and new forms of attack are being devised by attackers. This makes B, C and E correct.

202   C, E

Investigation and identification of the risks that DRF face satisfies identify all the issues.

Agreeing the programme objectives satisfies aim towards a well defined target.

The IT manager has created four alternative options and the board selecting one satisfies the risk resource trade off.

The IT manager working with HR regarding appraisals ensure motivation and that satisfies ensure sustained business engagement.

That leaves work out how best to deliver the new cyber security systems and developing a plan that aligns business and technology to be completed.

203   C

The aspect of the AIC Traid are availability, integrity and confidentiality.

The mirror site, patch management, DRP and BCP means they have robust processes in place to maintain availability of their online presence.

Using encryption and training on threats such as social engineering and maintaining good secure passwords helps with confidentiality

The lack of user access controls mean that the integrity of the data they hold could be compromised by either deliberate employee actions, or by someone accidentally amending customer records.

204   C

They have identified the sensitive information they hold and how it could be attacked, they have implemented forms of protection, they have response and recovery plans. This means they still need to consider how they will detect a breach.

Integrity is not one of the principles of the core in the NIST cybersecurity framework.

205   A

It is part of the technologies, connection types, service providers and delivery channels in the factors that have a significant effect on inherent cyber security risk in the main component of the report, the management's description.

Preparing a statement of applicability is part of the process towards becoming ISO27001 compliant.